Writing for Y<

"*Writing for Your Readers* is one of the best books on writing I have read, and is *the best* book I've ever read about reporting." —**WRITER'S DIGEST magazine**

"Whether your bent is toward becoming a novelist, historian or essayist, you will find *Writing for Your Readers* packed with tidbits, paragraphs and/or whole chapters that will enable you to sharpen your abilities. . . . If you feel the slightest inclination to be an author or reporter, then you can't afford to miss the opportunity of reading this book. But a word of caution. Don't borrow it from a friend or from the library. Buy it because you'll want to refer to it constantly." —**THE NEWS, Southbridge, Massachusetts**

"If more reporters would read this sensible book on writing, perhaps we'd all wince less often with our morning read." —**Michael Zielenziger, THE KANSAS CITY STAR**

"It has something to offer both the beginners and the experienced; it has specific ideas, something many writing books lack; and I like it too because it recognizes that the writing must come out of the reporting, and cannot be a substitute for the reporting." —**Professor Judith Serrin, Graduate School of Journalism, Columbia University**

"Packed with excellent suggestions for getting a solid grip on your non-fiction articles . . . this book both inspires and instructs." —**THE BAKERSFIELD CALIFORNIAN**

"Enlightening and refreshing . . . the chapters are . . . packed with a lot of helpful information." —**ROCKY MOUNTAIN NEWS**

"Anyone who ever writes anything can benefit richly from this stimulating, nuts-and-bolts book." —**SPRINGFIELD (Massachusetts) REPUBLICAN**

"A gunny sack stuffed with practical advice from a professional writing coach who knows something about the game . . . all of us can be much better at our trade than we are. All of us should be. This tells writers how they can be." —**TOPEKA (Kansas) CAPITAL JOURNAL**

Writing for Your Readers

Notes on the Writer's Craft
from The Boston Globe

Second Edition

by
Donald M. Murray

Old Saybrook, Connecticut

Library of Congress Cataloging-in-Publication Data

Murray, Donald Morison, 1924-
      Writing for your readers : notes on the writer's craft from the
Boston Globe / by Donald M. Murray. — 2nd ed.
   p. cm.
  Includes index.
  ISBN 1-56440-051-4
  1. Journalism—Authorship. I. Boston globe. II. title.
PN4781.M84 1992
808'.06607—dc20   92-12446
                               CIP

Manufactured in the United States of America
Second Edition/First Printing

For my First Reader,
Minnie Mae

CONTENTS

FOREWORD

The first time Don Murray ambled through the newsroom at the *Boston Globe* in the early 1980s, he taught me a lesson.

"I'll tell you who some of your good writers are," he said with that impish smile and twinkle in the eye.

"Who?" said I, taking the bait.

"Her. And him. And him. And her," he said, pointing discreetly.

"I didn't realize you knew them," I said.

"I don't," Murray chuckled.

"Well, then how do you know they are good writers?"

"Because," he said, "when they write, their lips move."

I haven't stopped learning from him since.

When I think back to the memorable periods when Murray was writing coach at the *Globe,* I have two images: The first is of Murray, the writer, sitting on a hard wooden bench outside my office as I arrive in the early morning to a virtually empty cityroom. Murray is scribbling in his daybook, his mind focused on a different time and a different place. He neither sees nor hears me until I am two feet away. Certainly if I were a writing coach, I would have been hastily preparing or polishing my presentation for the morning session. Not Don. He is on to his next book, his next poem, whatever. The day's lesson plan was organized and ready to go well before he arrived.

The second image I have is of Murray, the teacher, sitting on the rim of a square of tables with a dozen reporters gathered around. He gives a ten-minute opening statement, tightly targeted to the topic he has chosen for the seminar, and the next thing I know we are all writing—including Murray—fulfilling an exercise he has devised. "Write fast," he prods. "It's like riding a bicycle. You need velocity." Suddenly we are spinning out paragraphs of description, or trying ten ways to write the same central point to a story, or writing sentences that express tension between two poles. Then we are reading aloud and discussing. In a flash an hour and a half has passed.

As our writing coach, Murray had only one request: that the editor sit in and participate. It was like a bonus. It ranks among the most fun I have had as an editor.

This book is a way of putting the reader at that table, hearing the issues that were explored and *gaining* the wisdom of Murray's insightful thinking. It would be fruitless for me to attempt any kind of summary, but some of his lines still resonate in my mind:

"As a reporter: What surprised you? What are you learning? What was unexpected?"

"Corduroy writing is when you use quotes every three grafs."

"Some writers think color can be laid in like raisins in raisin bread, but it should be used *only* to progress the story."

"I like the word 'voice' rather than style, because style sounds like something you buy off a rack. When we say 'voice', we should mean the voice of the text, not the voice of the writer. Voice is flavor, voice is the music of writing matching the meaning of story."

"Judge a good story by the amount of information you throw away."

"Writing is one-on-one, not like TV announcing."

As you read this book, you will hear cogent lines like these from a man who eats, drinks, and thinks writing. You will be sitting at his elbow at that table. Like me, you will learn from what you hear.

"I say "hear," because Murray moves his lips when he writes.

JOHN S. DRISCOLL
Editor
The Boston Globe

Acknowledgments

I am, of course, indebted to all those writers and editors who have helped me to learn my craft, but I have special appreciation for Christopher Scanlan and Lisa Miller, who made special contributions—on deadline—that greatly improved this edition. I have been instructed by my editor Bruce Markot— my student who has become my teacher—and by Nina Maurer, copy editor, and Nancy Freeborn, designer.

Introduction:
THE WRITER IN THE
NEWSROOM

Today's newspaper readers know the news when they open their paper. The law is passed, the bank president charged, the baseball manager canned, the plane crashed, the stock market down, the number of AIDS patients up— the news has been delivered on radio and television but they read the paper to find out its significance. Readers don't read for what but for why; to discover what isn't and what may be; what if and how come; what's he or she really like; and, most of all, what does it mean to me?

The reporter—and writers must first be reporters—delivers the information and the writer shapes it into meaning. The skilled writer makes the news walk and talk; sets the scene; puts action, and inaction, into context; reveals motive and implication; weaves past, present, future into event; and does it on deadline with clarity and grace, accuracy and liveliness.

What the writer does can best be understood and therefore learned by examining the writing process. This book, which explores the process that produces accurate, graceful writing, is distilled from newsletters written for the editorial staff of the *Boston Globe* while I served two hitches as writing coach. The process approach to studying writing breaks down a craft that often appears mysterious and invisible into a sequence of activities. Every city room is crowded with writing critics who can describe in explicit terms what is wrong with a story but few who can describe what is right with another story. We all know what doesn't work when we read it but become inarticulate when we read a story that works.

The writing process places priority on what works: Why is this story good, and what stages did the writer pass through to make the final draft effective? Good writing is magic; but if you want to know magic, you have to talk to magicians. They repeat magic, producing the impossible on schedule, and so do our best writers. Researchers of the writing process observe and question the best writers on their best stories to discover what went right.

They discover an ever-evolving description of the basic process, of what most effective writers do most of the time. Of course the writing process changes according to the thinking and working style of the writer, although there is a remarkable similarity among most effective writers. The process also changes with the writing task and even more with familiarity with the writing task. The more we write a particular kind of story, the more we can anticipate problems and solve them in advance of writing. Nevertheless, it is possible to describe a basic writing process. The process in this book is different from what I have described in other books; it evolves from the study of newspaper writers and the conditions under which newswriters do their job.

The basic writing process on which this book is constructed is made up of six overlapping stages. They are:

Focus
Explore
Rehearse
Draft
Develop
Clarify

The chapters in this book are divided into these stages in the writing process and contain specific advice on how to improve in each part of the writing process; but the reader should never forget that the writer adapts the process to the writer's own working style, the writing task, the time and space available, and all the conditions that surround the writing of each story. The writer moves back and forth in the writing process, sometimes finding the focus during development, starting with rehearsal and moving back to focus, drafting to explore—writing is not a military operation but a craft of discovery and surprise.

A familiar, basic writing style allows the writer who is having difficulty to identify the problem and solve it on the spot. It gives the writer a way of improving the craft, of making use of the techniques of effective writers.

It also allows the editor to understand where the writer is in the writing process and to respond to a writer's work in a manner that is appropriate to that stage instead of responding as if every draft were final. And, as Joel Rawson, an instructive skeptic to my work who is now executive editor of the *Providence Journal,* pointed out, the writing-process approach gives writers and editors a language that allows them to communicate about the entire craft of writing, to describe what is right as well as what is wrong with a story, and to collect an inventory of writing techniques that have worked in the past and may apply to writing tasks in the future.

When your writing is going well, there is no need to be aware of the process; when it is not going well, it may be helpful to return to the process. Eventually you will graduate from our writing process to your own writing processes. You should do this by studying the writing processes of the best writers with whom you work, combining their lessons and our lessons into your own pattern—*when it is effective for you.* Most of all, look back at those times when your writing has gone well. Discover what works for you when faced with a particular task, what attitudes are important, what working conditions make it easy for you to produce good stories, what writing processes produced effective writing.

The reader depends on writers to make sense of their world, to provide at least what Robert Frost described as a "momentary stay against confusion." The reader needs writers who reveal, explain, entertain, persuade, and, most of all, articulate readers' own feelings and thoughts.

To be a writer in a newsroom is to have a high calling; the writer reveals the world to those living in it so that they can make sense of their lives. And in doing so, we enjoy the gift of first sight, the glimpse of pattern that explains our world to us. In using language to define our world we practice a craft that should give us many gifts—the gift of concentration, the gift of making, the gift of play. Few pleasures can compare with finding the right word, the defining phrase, or the clear, running sentence. The cliché that "easy writing makes hard reading" is not true. Easy writing makes easy reading.

Focus:
Find the Tension

The experienced writer sees the world through the lens of language, and that lens captures the tension between forces in the world that will produce a story. That tension may be between one individual and another; between a new idea and an old one; between an individual and society; between a belief and a newly discovered fact; between what is said and unsaid, seen and unseen; between the writer and the world; between what is being done and what should be done; between cause and effect, reality and illusion. The writer seeks the drama in the world.

The starting point is in conflict. It is not that bad news is good news, although any responsible newswriter or editor must carry a burden of guilt about that. The writer stands, notebook or tape recorder in hand, at the crossroads where the forces of the world may collide.

It is at these crossroads that the world changes, and it is the job of the newswriter to observe, document, relate, and connect;

to tell those affected by the collision that it is coming, that it is happening, that it has happened; to describe and predict the chain of action and reaction that results from each collision; and to reveal the individuals who are involved and how they cause change or are changed.

The dramatic interaction of people and forces is caught by the writer in a word, a phrase, a sentence, or a paragraph. The writer selects and narrows so that language, the writer's lens, makes what is at first only glimpsed come clear. Focus identifies and isolates a central tension or conflict so that it can be explored in writing. The vision is held and then developed, as idea becomes draft and draft becomes published story.

ONE

FINDING THE LINE

Writing my "Over Sixty" column made me realize there is a moment when I know have a column. That always-surprising moment arrives when I hear "the line."

Although I recognized this crucial point in my writing process while writing my column, I found that I had been depending on the line while writing articles, difficult letters, talks, poems, and books of fiction and nonfiction. The line is a fragment of language—sometimes a single word, often a phrase or series of words, rarely a sentence—that makes me follow it. It might be described as a question that demands an answer, an experiment that I must perform, an itch I must scratch, a path I must follow, a hint, a clue, or a vague shape I cannot make out but must.

Elements in a Line

The elements that exist (most of the time) in this linguistic trigger mechanism include:

Tension

A sense of forces headed for a collision (courtship?) or of forces exploding in opposite directions (marriage?).

Conflict

Irony, or a tension between what should be and what is. An energy that will be released by the writing of the story.

Play

The possibility of surprise, discover, contradiction, learning. The writing of the draft will teach me something I do not understand by knocking down the blocks of a previous meaning and stacking up the blocks of a new meaning.

Music

The sound of the voice *of the text.* This is my voice and more, the child of my voice, adapted to the purpose and audience of the to-be-written text. The rhythm or beat of music, the sound of what I will write, leads my writing ear towards meaning.

Form

A hint of the shape of the piece. Its length, pace, proportions. Not a rigid pattern but a territory to be explored—hill country or river valley, coast or plain—and a sense of the time it will take.

Ease

I never start without the illusion of ease, which may be false but often is not when I have found the line and follow it.

All of those elements are usually in the line, and they are so important for me that I will not start a draft, even on deadline, until I have found the line, the path of possibility. That is my starting point.

The Form of the Line

The line comes to me in many forms. Often it arrives in my head when I least expect it, but almost immediately it is written down in my daybook, a spiral notebook I keep near me most of the time, or on a scrap of paper. Other times it comes as I scribble in my daybook, more consciously thinking about what I may write. In either case, the scribbling is vital: Writing the line usually changes it in small but crucial ways that are constructive, and it starts to grow its own meaning. Writing the line preserves it; last week's line becomes this week's column.

I am going to share some of the lines that have worked for me because of their very ordinariness. The lines I share with you will not impress. This is private language, private notation. I hear the mystery and the music and the potential meaning in what is meaningless to others. If I am successful, I will turn it into public language and during the process I, the writer, and others, the readers, may experience the magic, the music, and the meaning.

But first I have to be able to hear and see what is not yet there. I have to be able to catch the vague shape of possible meaning, the hesitant, quiet sounds that may grow strong. The line appears to me in many forms:

Word

The word "playground" keeps appearing in my daybook. That single word contains significant tension for me because my family religion, combined with my native cowardice, made the playground a place of terror, testing, and failure. I will explore that word in a piece of writing someday.

The word "ghostwriter" has just ignited a revision of the novel I'm writing. It's a word I've often used for a trade I've practiced, but within the context of my evolving novel draft, it has a special and surprising resonance for me.

Fragment

This is the most common way the line appears to my ear or my eye. I read "I had an ordinary war" on my daybook page and started to pursue a novel. Obviously, the horror of war is what becomes ordinary. Other notebook fragments—"a teenager, I had enormous hands" and "hats. Bob becomes police reporter"—were the way recent columns began. The phrase "report from the front," which I "wrote" in my head during a heart attack, was scribbled in my daybook that morning, and that line started me on the column I wrote between the attack and bypass surgery.

The columns that have received the most reactions started with lines that contain good examples of tension: I heard myself saying on the phone, "I'm proud of my wrinkles," and knew I had a line and a column. Sitting in a bank parking lot I scribbled, "I didn't know it would be a full-time job to do nothing," and another line and column had arrived.

Image

In one unexpected moment I saw the way my mother kept the three places always set at the kitchen table ("the places at the kitchen table were always set") and as I captured that image in a poem, I recaptured the lonely silence of my home. The imagined image of the surgeons waving good-bye when I almost died between my bypass operations ("the doctors, happy in green, wave at my leaving") lead to another poem that was, at least, good therapy if not good poetry.

List

The list is a powerful thinking tool. When young children start making lists, we know they have made an enormous stride forward. My line is often a list:

touch
old
NY Times
hands in middle of night
football
parents' marriage bed

That lead to a column on touching—and more. All the elements on the list were in the column, although in a very different order. It was not an outline but a confusion of items that were significant to me and became ordered and meaningful through their writing.

Lead

I do not try to force a marriage between the line and the lead, but, of course, that relationship often develops. The line is the starting point for my written exploration. "I am not going to write a column about my daughter Hannah's wedding" became, of course, the lead from which the column grew. Many lines are shaped and developed in my head, in my daybook, or on my word processor until they become the lead. I am one of those writers who must have the lead before I go on, and I have come to realize that it is usually the line that gives me the lead.

Those are the most frequent forms of the line that come to me, but there are others, such as a quotation. A surgeon told me he was going to sit by the pool and write when he retired. I got back at him in a column. Often a fact, or the illusion of factualness, in a statistic or report finding will contain the acorn of a piece of writing. A revealing detail—the colonel who ordered one of our regiments to attack another was promoted to general and sent back to safety in England—may lead to an article, a story, an essay, or a book.

Pursuing the Line

Making use of the line is, for me, a strange form of pursuit that has taken me years to perfect and to grow comfortable using. It is not a chase. That's the first lesson.

I may have to force myself to my writing desk, but once there I have to relax, to become receptive to language, to write easily. I do not pursue the line as much as put a tail on it. I am the private dick following a suspect who may saunter through a shopping mall or race along a mountain road. My job is to stay in sight, out of sight. I follow language to see where it will take me, influencing the text as little as possible.

I write my first draft quickly and uncritically, allowing the text to tell me what it will say. I am stenographer more than maker.

Then, once I have a draft, I cut and add, shape, form, polish, and clarify. But it all begins with the line. That is where the text begins. I write as I draw, by following the line.

TWO

THE QUALITIES OF A GOOD STORY

The good writer is forever a student of writing, extending the writer's voice, learning techniques of craft, and attempting experiments in meaning.

It is a lonely business, but not a solitary one. Writers need colleagues, test readers, editors, and sometimes a writing coach who, like the opera star's coach, does less teaching than reminding.

The old definitions of hard news—the story that has to be printed today—and the feature—the story that can wait until tomorrow—do not cover the diversity of stories printed in today's daily newsmagazine. But whatever the form or the subject, any good story has at least seven elements.

Information

Information, not language, is the raw material from which effective writing is built. The writer must collect specific, accurate pieces of information to be able to write effective prose. Too many stories and columns are written instead of reported; they are created by tricks of rhetoric when they should be constructed from a pattern of concrete detail. The revealing details that mark an exceptional story rarely come from competitors' stories, the telephone, or staring thoughtfully across the city room. Information that reveals is collected with the legs.

Significance

Good stories affect the reader. They threaten the reader's life, health, wealth, or sense of values. They give information the reader needs to know. They tell what has happened, what is happening, and what may happen. We should not, however, confuse significance with notoriety, doing stories on the rich, the famous, the powerful, and no one else. It is our duty to show the significance in material that at first appears insignificant.

Focus

The stories that newspaper writers usually take most pride in are long and often come in a series. The newswriter is a territorial animal with a primitive instinct to use up as much newsprint as possible. But the stories that survive are usually short, precisely limited, and clearly focused. Most good stories say one thing. They tell not of a battle, but of a soldier; they talk not about governance, but about a deal; they discuss not a socioeconomic group, but a person and a life.

Context

The effective story is put into perspective so the reader knows where the story has come from, where it is going, and how widespread or how typical it is. Sometimes the writer who is not very skillful delivers the context in a big, hard-to-swallow capsule in about, say, the third paragraph. The more skillful writer weaves the context through the story.

Faces

We should never forget that people like to read about people. Journalism presents ideas by introducing the reader to the people who are creating the ideas or by showing the people who are affected by them. For ideas, read laws, trends, scientific discoveries, judicial opinions, economic developments, international crises. News stories work best when the writer has the skill to get out of the way and allow the reader to meet and hear the people in the story.

Form

An effective story has a shape that both contains and expresses the story. A narrative will work if it has all the information the reader needs and if the story can be revealed in a chronological pattern of action and reaction.

The writer must find a form that gives the reader a satisfying sense of completion, a feeling that everything in the story flows toward an inevitable conclusion.

Voice

Memorable news stories create the illusion of an individual writer speaking aloud to an individual listener. A good newspaper is filled with fascinating conversations. But the writer must remember to keep the voice appropriate to the story. We all know writers who use the same voice every time they write. There is always an Uncle Elmer who bellows in the same way at a football game, wake, Thanksgiving dinner, and in a hospital room. The good writer seeks a voice that is consistent throughout the story but varies its volume and rhythm to the meaning. And we should never forget that even in an age of mass communication the act of reading is private, one writer speaking to one reader.

THREE

THE CONDITIONS THAT ENCOURAGE WRITING

We are taught that we learn to write by the elimination of error. That is the second half of the story. The most important learning comes from identifying our effective writing and repeating it. Part of the repeating comes from knowing the conditions that make effective writing possible and encouraging those conditions on future stories.

Need

The desert war calls up my own war memories—and guilts I must confront—in writing. A story works best for me if I have a personal need to explore the subject, and I will try to turn an assignment so that I can learn something a reader will also need to know.

Habit

Nulla dies sine linea. I do not wake, singing, "To writing, to writing, I will go." I drag my rump to the desk by habit. Most of the time I like being there, but I never like going there.

Tools

I just started my eightieth daybook in which I make notes and practice some of the writing that must come before writing. I also found as I lived out of town for a month just how dependent I have become on *my* computer, *my* software, *my* hard disk.

Attitude

If it isn't fun, I won't do it. Fortunately the writer, even the staff writer on deadline, has considerable control over the writing or how the writing is done. I make a game of writing: I'll try this one without looking at my notes, I'll see if I can write the crazy way the editor suggested, I'll write the end first, I'll try to write faster than usual or more slowly. Writing is too serious a business to be taken seriously. Good writing is the product of play.

Limitations

I am stimulated by a deadline and I set the deadline ahead of need—my column is delivered the Monday of the week before it will be published on Tuesday. And I play daily deadline games: "I'll finish this section of the book before Don Graves comes by to go to lunch." I also need a sense of spatial limitations (an 800-word column, an 80,000-word novel, a twelve-line poem) to plan as well as pace my draft.

Experiment

I have a private experiment on each writing project. I'll try the present tense, or emphasize visual images, or depend on dialogue that keeps me interested in a type of story I have written many times before. It clarifies the meaning in a way it is not usually clarified and sharpens my writing skills.

Process

I have ways of writing that seem to work for me and I follow my own rituals.

Reporting. Good writing depends on—and stimulates—awareness. I need an abundance of information, far more than I can use, so that I can draw on a large inventory of information, experience, observation, and feelings.

Rehearsal. I write fragments in my head and in my daybook until the subject achieves a certain ripeness. (A deadline accelerates the rehearsal and the ripening process.)

Lead. Not all writers have to have the lead first, but I have to have, at least, a working lead that I believe will be the final one. The beginning sentence may establish the tone, content, point of view towards the content, and the direction of the piece.

Voice. Not just my voice, but my voice adapted to meaning, the situation of the piece, and its intended audience; *the voice of the text.* If I do not hear a voice I think appropriate, I will change the content to fit the voice or abandon the piece. I write by ear and it is the voice that keeps me going.

Spine. A sense of direction, a trail to explore, a sequence of information that leads me, and the reader, toward meaning.

Speed. I have to write fast to outwit the censor, to get enough velocity on the text so that I write what I do not expect, to cause the accidents that make my writing interesting to me and perhaps to my readers.

Readers

After a draft is finished, I need test readers. I use my wife and writing colleagues who stimulate me to have a new vision of my draft and who pass my personal test: When I leave them I want to write.

Editors

I need an experienced editor who can read my text in the context of my purpose and my voice, something that is not easy to find in the book business (I have just had four new editors during the writing of a new edition of one book). At the *Globe* I am blessed with Evelynne Kramer, who reads with a tough, critical eye—she has a sharper, more analytical eye than I have—but likes my writing and understands what I am trying to do. She responds to my drafts with questions, giving me room to read, reconsider, and repair my text.

Publication

I need the stimulus of publication. Nothing motivates me more than acceptance, publication, and praise. Give me any of the above and I start to think of new things to write about and new ways of writing about them.

FOUR

Interview:
DAVID MEHEGAN

When I am at the *Globe* I always enjoy stopping by David Mehegan's desk to chat about writing. He is articulate about our craft, and I learn from what he has to say about how effective writing is made.

David was born in Boston and grew up in the city and in Scituate. He earned a degree in English and Journalism at Suffolk University and intended to go into broadcasting; but the opportunities came in print journalism, and he realizes now he was better suited to that anyway. The story of his road to journalism may be instructive to those who want to find a job in hard times: the road is rarely clear or straight but if you hone your talent through a variety of jobs, the break may come.

The first opportunity Mehegan had was as copy boy at the *Boston Herald Traveler* while in college in the late sixties, ripping wire copy and getting coffee. As David reports,

> On that paper, an office boy (and we were all addressed as "boy," no matter how old we were) could get a tryout on the staff after a certain number of years. But the paper closed in March or April 1972 and I missed my chance. I was asked to write an inside story on the death of the *Herald* for *Boston Magazine* in June 1972, which brought me:
>
> (1) $250,

   (2) a plug in Frazier's column,

   (3) a million-dollar libel suit (settled out of court), and

   (4) by means too complicated to explain, a job as a college text book editor at Houghton Mifflin Company.

After two years of penury at Houghton Mifflin, editing books like *Fundamentals of Counseling* and *The Later Renaissance in England: Nondramatic Prose and Poetry, 1600–1660* and, believe it or not, a textbook on newswriting that is still in use, I went to the University of Massachusetts for more money and less stimulation as an assistant secretary to the Board of Trustees. During both of those jobs, I was working weekends at the *Globe* as a copy editor.

In 1976, Anne Wyman hired me to edit the letters column and do layout and copyediting on the editorial page. After three years and 35,000 letters, I became assistant magazine editor under Mike Janeway. Two years later, in 1981, Al Larkin went from magazine writer to magazine editor, succeeding Janeway, and I took his spot as writer. I was a staff magazine writer for three years, then went back to the Night Desk for one year. I went to the City Desk as a general assignment reporter in 1985, then joined the Suburban Team, then went to the Business section in 1987 to cover the retailing beat, then became assistant book editor in 1991.

David was interviewed when he was doing a superb job covering the retail business in the Business section.

How do you prepare for an interview?

I need to know enough about what I'm writing about so that I don't ask questions that make me look foolish and so that I have a chance of understanding the person I'm talking to. But I do not worry about being ignorant because my theory is that we are all professional ignoramuses; it's our job not to know something and then to find out.

Do you have any special techniques for face-to-face interviews?

No techniques, except to approach them with sensible curiosity, to treat people courteously, to show intense attention, and to try to respond deftly and intelligently with unprepared questions when the subject says surprising or unexpected things. Most people distrust and dislike reporters, but if they feel they can trust you, they will freely tell their story. I take notes and almost never use a tape. For me, every interview is a stumbling, mumbling thing.

How do you get people to answer questions they don't want to answer?

Again I think trust is the key. Sometimes people can't answer a question, but more often they are afraid of what you're going to do to them in print. I give off-the-record assurances freely, probably more freely than most reporters, and always keep that commitment. What you lose in juicy quotes you often gain in deepened understanding, which is much the more important thing in the long run. You want to build a reputation for being a straight-shooter. If you prove trustworthy, they will be more talkative next time. Getting information from liars and other unsavory people is a separate problem.

How do you collect the revealing details that make a story clear and lively? What do you look for when reporting a story?

Collecting details is not difficult; seeing them often is. One has to be alert to pick up anything that is funny, poignant, startling, or beautiful. Unexpected discoveries are the raw material of vitality in a story. I look for any detail that makes that story different from any other. William F. Homer, Jr., (*Herald* financial editor and my first journalism professor) used to repeat ad nauseam, "Individualize by specific detail."

When you have a complicated story, do you have any techniques that help you understand it?

I just write it. That helps me understand it.

When you're covering the same beat over a period of time, as you are these days, how do you keep from going stale? It's my judgment that you haven't gone stale.

I think I am extremely stale, but sometimes I think that may not be entirely a bad thing. In covering a beat, particularly a business beat, it is easy to become fascinated with a subject as you become more knowledgeable about it, and to begin to make the fatal supposition that everybody finds this stuff as interesting as you do. We've all encountered the guy at the party who drones on about the wholesale coat-hanger business.

I hate malls and stores and shopping, and I tend to think, "God, this is boring stuff; surely my readers think so, too. There must be something I can do to make this interesting." This leads to twists and variations and odd leads, which are all to the good.

An example that comes to mind at the moment was a recent story about Caldor, the department store, which I started by quoting Admiral Jellicoe at the Battle of Jutland. I don't know if that worked, but it came from my saying to myself, "There must be some new way to get people to read about this."

Do you outline, organize your notes, etcetera?

No, I minimize rituals that delay the actual writing. I do push all the other crap out of the way. Sometimes I make a simple list of elements that must not be left out.

I've been concerned about lead writing recently. What do you try to do in a lead, how do you try to do it?

I try to do in the lead [the post–hot metal spelling!] what I try to do throughout a story, which is always to speak directly to the reader's desire for interest and enjoyment. I'll use any trick that will work, as long as it makes the reader go on to the next paragraph.

I try not to write the conventional who-what-when-where lead that we all learned in Journalism 101 because I believe that in most cases that lead makes dull, and sometimes difficult, reading. There isn't much point in cramming all that information in the first sentence if it produces an unreadable sentence. Sometimes you must write it that way, of course.

While you're drafting a story, what do you concentrate on?

I concentrate on continuous logical transition from one point to another, from lead to the end. A story should move well, like an actor on stage. Put another way, it should be a chain, rather than a stack, of facts. I also concentrate on writing strictly to length. I do not want my stories trimmed or bitten because I have overwritten. And I care about endings. I think a story should end and not simply stop.

Will you say something about voice? How do you hear and tune your voice?

I don't know about hearing and tuning, but I would say that I try to write every story with such a voice and tone that the reader is aware that there is a person on this side of the keyboard. I want it to sound like me, to the degree that is possible.

It's easy to forget that newswriting is a convention-bound literary form with its own argot, and most stories read like they could have been written by a newswriting software package. Without being excessively colloquial, I try to tell the story as I would if I were telling it to someone standing next to me at a bar or at a party. We ought to remember that we are storytellers, not just researchers, and every storyteller must develop a voice. When people say of one of my stories, "I would have known that was you, even if it hadn't had your name on it," I feel that I am succeeding.

Clearly, though, I'm not talking about your "Pope shot" or "Plane crashes, 230 die" type stories, where the reader demands raw facts as fast and as clean as possible. When news happens at 5:00 p.m., who can think about voice?

What is the writer's task as you see it?

After putting facts on the public record, I think our task is to help the reader find his or her way through the facts, to help the reader make sense of them. So the whole story, from first sentence to last—in the way we organize it, in the way we use faces and voices, in the tone we take, in the facts we use, in the overt analysis we venture to offer—should reflect our intelligent understanding, which we give to the reader.

I think we should be intelligent in our approach to what we do, not in the sense of braininess, but in the sense of espionage: the capacity to take in and interpret information.

I also think we should try to entertain whenever possible, to give good reading, using style and eyes for detail, without going so fatally overboard that we are attracting the reader's attention to us rather than to our story.

What are the three problems you face most frequently in writing? How do you solve them?

First, getting started. Second, getting into the story everything I think should be there. Third, assembling the story so that it has integrity and logic. (A fourth problem is working conditions: the infernal racket and crowding in the newsroom, which may bother me more than most people.)

Number one: I get started by fiddling around and procrastinating so long that terror of failing to produce a story forces my fingers to start rattling away. I don't believe I have ever failed to produce a story that I was committed to, though each day I think, surely this will be the day.

Number two: I often make a list of points-that-must-not-be-omitted-no-matter-what, and I make space for those points.

As for number three, good assembly for me is largely a matter of revision.

What is your process of revision and editing? Do you have your own private checklist? If so, what is it?

Revision is a grand term for the frantic process of fixing the mess, which is usually all there is time for. There's no checklist except for the don't-leave-out list. I just keep reading the story, first on the tube, then in paper form, usually standing up at a file cabinet far from my desk, tinkering and tinkering, shifting paragraphs around, throwing out words, shortening sentences, worrying and fretting, checking spellings and job titles and numbers. I try to look at the copy intensely, as I did when I was an editor, operating on the assumption that any mistake I miss will get in the paper. I never say, "So-and-so will catch it." So-and-so won't.

What advice do you have for beginning writers?

With respect to writing, I guess it would be to write clear, straight, fresh, active sentences with as many aggressive verbs as possible, and to avoid conventional journalistic writing.

What are the three things that editors can do that are most destructive for you?

I have never known a truly destructive editor. An editing change that alters the meaning in an important way or introduces an error (which has happened to me, though not in the Business section) would be a destructive change. But that does not happen if editors communicate with writers. You have to encourage them to do that by being responsive to their questions and telling them to call you at home. I like to be called at home and I thank editors for calling me with a question, no matter how the question is resolved.

What are the three things that editors can do that are most helpful for you?

I suppose it would be to read closely and respond thoughtfully. Fix what is obviously wrong. Raise with me any concern or doubt so that we can eliminate problems.

What can a writer do to develop an effective relationship with an editor?

You can encourage able editors to do their best work by treating them and the editing process with respect. As difficult as writing is, if an able editor can help, I can't imagine that anyone wouldn't want that help. Also, I think you should raise complaints or grievances directly with the editor, in a civilized way, if you think a principle is at stake. Some people would rather smolder and bitch to their neighbors.

What advice do you have for a beginning editor?

Presumably a beginning editor would be a copy editor. My advice to a copy editor is to read it again, and one more time, if you can, and to ask questions fearlessly. Do not be intimidated when your questions are unwelcome, as they frequently will be, even by other editors. Also, remember the medical principle: "Above all, do no harm."

What books, authors, and publications have you found helpful as a writer that you would recommend to other people on the Globe *staff?*

It is the books of writing, rather than those about writing, that have meant the most to me. Paul Hemphill is a writer I admire, along with E. B. White's essays, most of the time. John Updike's critical writing is to me a model of fairness and clarity, although I don't like his fiction much. Tuchman's and Manchester's books. William Maxwell and William Trevor. Amos Elon. Flora Lewis.

Do you have favorite Globe *writers?*

Not exactly favorites, but some I always read without restlessness. Alan Lupo for wit, clarity, toughness, compassion and good reporting. Curtis Wilkie and Joan Vennochi for a good seamless blend of reporting and interpretation (and consistent high quality overall). Dick Knox for thoroughness, clarity, and dedication to quality. Susan Trausch, Richard Saltus, Dick Dyer, Bob Taylor, Dave Greenway, Dave Wilson. Many others.

FIVE

Interview:
RICHARD SALTUS

As a reader who staggered through biology, chemistry, and physics at North Quincy High School, learning little and retaining less, I am impressed when writers can make such material interesting and clear. As a writer who did some magazine medical reporting, I know how hard that task can be.

I have been impressed by Richard Saltus and have interviewed him so that we can all learn how he works.

Where do you get story ideas?

From journal articles, news releases, and meetings about various areas of science. From scientists whom I'm interviewing about something else. Occasionally from editors who suggest we expand on a previous story or work up a series on a broader aspect of areas we've covered. Often, by looking back at two or three stories I've written on a particular subject and seeing a pattern or logical follow-up.

The best ideas sometimes spring up in conversations with people entirely outside of science, readers, for example, who are curious about something, who have a friend or relative working on an interesting project, or who think we have missed the boat on a story that's already been in the paper and needs another angle. And, as on every other beat, there are natural stories: when shuttles are launched, Nobel Prizes won, nuclear accidents, new species discovered.

How do you make assignments your own?

This is usually a problem only when it's a story that has already been done by another paper, magazine, or network. Aside from the unconscious, personal selection of subject matter that every reporter does, I usually ask myself, do I feel there is some level of accuracy or truth that seemed missing in the previous treatment? Have there been new developments? Was there an obvious bias? And, perhaps most important, after dipping into the reporting for awhile, are there aspects that speak to me in a way that didn't get much attention before?

What clues tell you that you have a good idea?

When I look into the story and it opens up farther and deeper, rather than seeming to exhaust itself quickly, I feel I'm on the right track. The best feeling is seeing a number of pieces of a story converge into something coherent, and looking in the clips, and the *Readers' Guide* and finding almost nothing on it. I am less influenced than I used to be by what other reporters or editors think, although I don't discount it because in retrospect some of the best stories have been ones that I only had a hint of (and other people no idea at all) until I had done a fair amount of reporting.

What reporting techniques have you developed that you wish you had known when you began reporting?

At the Associated Press, editors used to say that if you were any good, you could go report on something without having read a word on it. I didn't really believe it then, but now I'm even more aware of how important it is to know the lay of the land, to be as prepared as you can, before doing important interviews. On the other hand, there is something to be said for plunging in and starting to talk to a few people right away. But you can be sorry you weren't better informed if you interview crucial sources while you're still learning the background of a story.

In the past, I sometimes avoided the most obvious or oft-quoted sources because I suspected they would be unavailable, wouldn't talk, or wouldn't have anything new to say. I have since learned that often there is a good reason why certain people are quoted over and over. Not only are some people inherently more quotable, but there are sources who simply are always better informed, keep up with developments, and understand how to communicate with the press—and often they are easier to reach than you'd think.

What interviewing techniques have you developed? How do you prepare for an interview? What climate do you attempt to establish? How do you take notes? What are your favorite questions?

I'm not conscious of many techniques as such. I suppose I try to get a sense of whether a subject is one who has his spiel already composed and just needs you to get out of the way, let him tell it, and then go back after particular questions. Some subjects need to be drawn out in dialogue form. I prepare by trying to know at least what has been written about the source or story in the mass media, or maybe in specialized places, too. If the person is exceptionally busy, or if I'm more than usually uninformed about the subject, I will write down some questions to make sure the interview is efficient.

With scientists, it's important to establish how up-to-speed I am on a topic, because that influences the entire shape of the interview. For me, the trick is to be as well informed as possible but to be in a frame of mind that more closely resembles the casual reader. That way, I hope to avoid missing the obvious big questions. One difficulty in establishing a climate is allowing your natural curiosity and fascination with a story to interfere with the detachment, even suspicion, that sometimes is necessary. If I fail at this, sometimes I'll be sorry later on because I may have been taken in or duped.

I don't have many favorite questions, but I admired one reporter who always posed everything in superlatives—"What's the biggest, best, worst, most important," and so forth—which can elicit good quotes. I usually ask scientists why they got interested in whatever it is they're doing. This is often important to the story and sometimes reveals something interesting about the person.

What kind of information do you try to get in your notebook that will make the writing go well?

If there's time, I try to fill in around quotes and notes things that remind me of the context, so that if sentences are fragmented or illegible,

I have a chance of reconstructing them. If the interview is for a profile or a scientist-in-the-workplace type of story, I look around and jot down anything about the environment that helps create a sense of the person: things written on a blackboard, items relating to the subject's life away from the office, clothing, notes from associates—it's all fair game. When a strong or unexpected emotion accompanies a quote, I'll try to get that down. I also try to jot little subheads or summaries of where we are in the interview if there's time, so I can find things more quickly; this also helps with the aforementioned illegible notes, of which I have more than my share.

What kind of rehearsing or preparation for writing do you do during the reporting, or between the reporting and the writing?

Depends on the magnitude of the story. When I have gathered a lot of material for a big piece, I sometimes talk the story through with a friend (or stranger), who very often asks logical questions I have neglected to answer.

Many times I am surprised at what other people find more or less interesting in something I've been working on, and that may influence how I order the elements of the piece. From time to time I will try out leads in a spare moment, or nut graphs, or second graphs—just pieces of things that help me to know if I'm ready to write or still floundering. Occasionally, when the story is one that reminds me of the work of a writer I admire, I'll dip into his or her writing to remind me about the tone that person used, writing tricks that seemed to fit well with that subject.

How do you prepare to write? What do you do with your notes? Do you outline, and if so, how?

I have no regular method of overcoming the resistance to getting started. I don't always clean up my desk and pay the bills first, but sometimes it's part of the process. Usually I read over all my notes and underline things I plan to use. Sometimes I start a laundry list on a file in the VDT of things I want to be sure not to leave out. Then I put all my notes on a clipboard (I used to use file folders, but they inevitably ended up all over my desk and the floor).

On a story of any size, I'll try to outline by putting down single sentences, each with one idea (they tend to run into more if I don't watch out) that get me through at least half the story. It's rare that I can outline an entire story before losing patience and plunging in, but if I can get the top organized, I'm relatively happy. I've read about outline systems where people jot down ideas at random positions on a piece of paper and connect them in all kinds of different ways, but that's never really worked for me. Often, I'll write, say, the first 25 percent of a story and then print it out and use that as the beginning of an outline, to sort of hurl me along in some direction with enough momentum to outline the rest of it.

How do you find the lead? How do you look for a lead, or what do you look for in a lead?

That's very difficult to do or to describe. The most important thing in the first lead I settle on is that it have the tone (or voice, if you prefer) that I'm aiming for. That's more important than the right content or the right idea, even. It has to evoke the effect I want the story to have—formal, conversational, dramatic, technical, skeptical, humorous, flippant, apocalyptic, heart-rending, whatever. That may come through an appropriate quote, a summing-up, or a set-up for suspense. Many times a visual image is where I start, whether it's the ambience of a laboratory, the main subject's gesture, or the look of a piece of technology.

More often than not, though, the lead I come up with this way doesn't survive revision, especially if it's a long and complex story, because by the time I get to the end the lead isn't right anymore.

How do you write? Slow? Fast? Do you listen to the text?

The pace depends a lot on the mood of the moment. On one story, I have to extract every word out of nowhere, going back again and again; on another, I may write almost as fast as I can type until I hit a slow spot. The latter is usually best, by far, even if it takes a lot of revision. Even when I have outlined, getting the organization to work requires a lot of tailoring to get the transitions smooth, and I tend to do that as I go along. So, the bottom line is probably that I write slowly, unless on deadline.

Listening is very, very important to me, especially in leads, but all the way through. If the cadence isn't right, it's hard for me to go on. I don't consciously read aloud and listen, but the sentences ring in my ear.

There's a tendency for sentences to get monotonously similar in a long story if I don't take time to break them up as I go along. It depends on what I've been reading, too: A writer who effectively uses simple, short sentences will get me trying to do that. At other times, I'll be enamored of long sentences with phrases that unroll this way and that and paragraphs made up of a nicely balanced combination of fluid and punchy sentences.

What are your three greatest writing problems and their solutions?

Organization. This just takes constant work, trial and error. I naturally prefer a more magazine-like organization where the material flows logically, building up and letting down but always with a leaning toward the end. Newspapers, though, call for front-loading the story with the best stuff. Editors like everything mentioned or teased up high, then explained at greater length later on. This tends to be hard to do without confusing the reader because of switching back and forth among different elements; as the story goes on, you have to pick up the teased points and weave them in. I think this is really difficult, but editors and readers don't seem to have the patience for the other method. About the only solution is revision. Once in a while I find an organizational scheme in someone else's writing and try to apply it to mine.

Being natural. Newswriting has its boilerplate and its clichés, and science writing has another whole set of stock phrases on top of that. You have to keep being aware of worn-out wordage and fight, all the time, against the lazy approach.

The last third of the story. For some reason there's often a point where the energy of the beginning and middle expends itself but there is more to say. Probably because of having written so much in pyramid style, I think my stories tend to get out of control or lose focus toward the end, instead of gathering themselves for a final push that carries the reader to a strong conclusion. I suppose one remedy is trying to write this part first, but I can't say that I have put this into practice very often.

What do you do when you get stuck?

I have to avoid the temptation to take it from the top again, though sometimes this can vault me over the trouble spot. On an important or long story, there's usually time to pack it in for the night and try the next day. Being stuck on a lead is the worst, because I don't like to go out and then return, no matter what the advice books say. If I can get a "goodenough" lead, though, that will allow me to continue and then improve the lead later. One thing I have learned about getting stuck, drugs are not the answer.

How do you read your own draft? How do you revise? How do you edit?

Over the years, I've come to accept the truth that I rarely can get a good draft in one try. The more I revise, usually, the better it gets—and by a lot, not a little. In fact, I've come to like revising. After a day of sitting with your nose a foot from the tube in intense concentration, I am amazed at what things I see after dinner, and maybe after a glass of wine, when I pick up that printout and give it a fresh look. Obvious bad organizational choices jump out, transitions that make no sense, things that worked well—everything seems much clearer then. I like to go over the draft then, marking sections that need to go up or down or out. It's a good time to show the piece to someone else, if possible.

Then, in the morning, I make the changes in the VDT text but try to keep from doing major rewriting at that point, especially if the story isn't finished.

No matter at what point I turn in a story, my editor usually has a lot of ideas for changes or cuts. We happen to work well together: If we have a fair amount of time and the story is a major one, he'll edit my writing and add some of his own, and then I'll rewrite his rewriting and add some of my own, and after a few cycles of this, including some arguments, we tend to be in good agreement.

How has your writing changed recently?

I'm not sure that my writing has changed all that much in the past few years, but I have a sense that it has become a little easier. As in many things, it may be that relaxing one's standards of what is acceptable quiets the harsh self-editor somewhat. This makes it easier to go on to the next paragraph, and the next one, without getting stuck. I'm sure I have benefited from the idea of getting something down and then revising it rather than insisting on a close-to-publishable text the first time.

On the other hand, I think I am more cautious about an off-the-wall lead that seems catchy but may be embarrassing when I look back at it later. If this means I am less experimental, that's not good. It probably means I get more stories done, though. I hope that in writing science stories I've become a little more conversational, because I have made an effort to replace jargon words with phrases that are more explanatory and helpful to the nonscientist.

How can an editor help you? How can an editor hurt you?

It's a delicate balance, without question. A good editor can tell you when an organizational strategy doesn't work, but of course this doesn't mean you will always agree with him or her. At an earlier stage in putting a story together, an editor can help a writer to focus his inchoate ideas. It's a bad idea to become too dependent on this, however, both because it can make the writer lazy and because it erodes the writer's independence of thought. After all, the focus may be the wrong one. It's a rare editor, but a welcome one, who can point out problems of wording, style, organization, etcetera and yet trust the writer to revise the text himself. Some editors have a hard time keeping their own writing out of the story. They may in fact have good substitutes for the original wording, but I think the story should be told as much in the writer's language as possible.

This is where a good editor can become bad. A writer who has every lead rewritten, every unconventional approach turned down and every story reorganized will lose confidence and become resentful. In my opinion, better to let some stories go without drastic editing (as long as they are in decent shape and accurate) than to destroy the writer's belief that he or she can produce a piece that is satisfactory.

At the same time, a bad editor is one who lets every story by a writer go through without engaging it in terms of content and style. When a writer gets used to having no editing, it can either make him careless or feel that he has no one helping him improve, no one to differentiate between what he's doing well and what needs work. This is a bad thing.

What advice do you have for a beginning reporter/writer on the Globe?

Write for different editors and sections when you have the opportunity. Don't let one editor, if you should be having trouble, get you down. Be willing to listen to and go along with suggestions, though, because there are many people here who have a lot to offer.

Take as much initiative as you can. Always be thinking of stories to do, angles of running stories to take off on.

Be aware of the fact that although there is some competition with other media in Boston, the *Globe* stands apart, and for that reason you may not get much feedback. In other words, you may not frequently be asked why you did something the way you did, how you could have done it better, or what you think about the way reporter X or Y did it at newspaper Z? Supply your own stimulation in that respect or get colleagues to give you feedback.

Remember that the *Globe* has many places where a writer/reporter can fit in. If the current assignment or beat is causing you a lot of grief, keep in mind that people shift around a lot and a better match may be down the road.

What books on writing have you found helpful? What writers do you admire and learn from?

I can't say that many "how-to" books are much good, unless one needs help with proper usage. One exception is *Writing with Power* by Peter Elbow, which contains a lot of good exercises and hints on organizing, dividing your time, getting looser, etcetera. I keep in my desk a folder with a bunch of examples of writing given to me by someone years ago who had it in a class. It has commentary about how they do what they do. I find it good to peruse when I'm stuck.

Writers I look to for inspiration or models include Didion, McPhee, Halberstam, Jeremy Bernstein, Lewis Thomas, the *Time* institutional style, the *New York Times* institutional style, or whoever had a good piece in the *Globe* today.

Explore:
Report for Surprise

The best writers seek surprise, delight in what they do not expect to see. They come to the story with a focus, an expectation, but they treasure the contradiction, the traitor fact, the quotation that goes against the grain, the unexpected that reveals.

Unfortunately, journalists (editors and reporters) usually see what they expect to see—even if it isn't there. The news appears to be predictable as you cover the flood of information that flows through the city room day after day after day. Patterns are discovered, and those patterns make it possible to control and communicate the flow, but it is easy to see patterns that are no longer there or to see the patterns gestating below the surface of the flood, the ones that will dominate the future. We saw the all-powerful Russian menace when it was weak, collapsing in upon itself; we did not see the significance of AIDS, and when it became significant we attempted to contain it to one small segment of our population.

In exploring the focus a writer looks for what isn't there as much as what is, hears the unsaid as well as the said, perceives "What if . . . ?"

The best reporter/writer is comfortable with discomfort and hears music in dissonance. Graham Greene once asked, "Isn't disloyalty as much the writer's virtue as loyalty is the soldier's?"

SIX

SEEING THE OBVIOUS

One problem editors and writers share is how to get ideas. The reader's appetite for fresh stories is never satisfied, and as soon as you get an idea it's gone. Following are fourteen techniques for developing new ideas and a discussion of what to do with them.

A good way to measure the vigor of a newspaper is to count the number of good stories that were not produced by the calendar, the police radio, the competitor's newspaper, the publisher's second cousin, or the PR release.

1. An editor once said that a good reporter "is forever astonished at the obvious." Inventory the obvious. List what is happening to you: your feelings, satisfactions, worries, wants, anxieties, hobbies, needs. You are a reader as well as a writer. Look for story ideas among the things that are changing your world and the world of those about you. Where's the money going? Where's the time going? Where's the fat going? What makes people laugh or get mad? What are people buying or not buying? How are they entertaining? What changes are taking place or not taking place in your family and on your street?

2. Brainstorm. You can do this alone or with a partner. You can do it with no goal in mind to see what ideas are dredged up, or with a goal such as how we should cover the election this year. The important thing is to suspend the censor, be willing to be silly, and just list specifics. For example:

- Crime
- Jail
- Bail

- More bail jumpers in a recession?
- Different crimes in a recession?
- Different criminals?
- Check 1932 police records.
- Talk to retired detective.
- Interview Prohibition detective.
- Changes in bail business.
- Pot smugglers compared to Prohibition smugglers.
- Used to be illegal bootleggers in the city. Still?
- Women treated differently from men on bail?
- Are people bailing out of yachts?
- Don't think so. Expensive yachts backordered at Boothbay. Story?
- Who's buying?
- Plus—$100,000 houses selling best in our town. How come?
- People paying cash.
- Remember wealth during the Great Depression.
- Plus—$100,000 houses selling for cash.
- Who's got the cash?

That's just a quick start on a brainstorming list that goes off in several different directions and circles back through itself. It's the best way of telling you what story ideas you already have stored in your brain. Brainstorming mobilizes memory and the subconscious. Once you have a brainstorming list look for items that surprise you and circle them. Then look for the items that connect and draw lines between them.

3. Try mapping instead of brainstorming or outlining. Mapping is a technique used in British schools that allows many people to explore a subject more effectively than they can by traditional outlines. Those who are interested in right-hemisphere brain techniques believe this approach reproduces the way in which the more creative parts of the brain work. Put the topic in the center of the page in an oval, and then as quickly as possible draw lines out that follow the ideas that occur to you. On the previous page is a five-minute mapping on a common journalism subject.

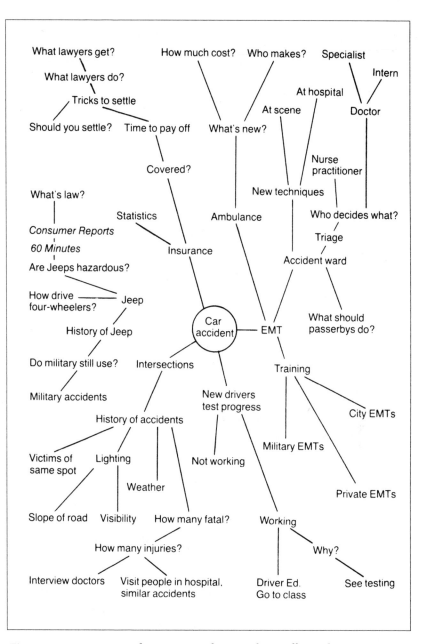

Five-minute mapping technique to explore a subject effectively.

4. Change your point of view. Drive to work by a different route. Go to a familiar place at an hour when you're not usually there. Shop in a supermarket patronized by people on welfare. Stand in line at an unemployment office and listen to what people are saying. Sit in a waiting room at a hospital clinic. Watch the ballgame from the bleachers. See point of view diagram below.

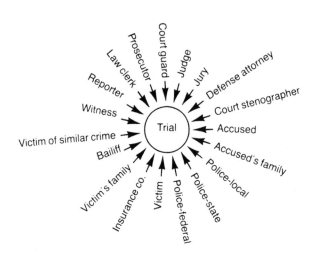

Point of view diagram. *Make a circle revealing the many points of view from which one story can be seen.*

5. Pursue an interest that forces you to see the world from a new point of view. Sketch, paint, take pictures. I draw, and to sketch an island I have to see that island—or that person, or that chair—more intensely than I have ever seen it before. I have to understand how that island was created and how trees manage to grow from the crevices in the rock; I have to know the bone structure within the face to reveal the face; I have to know how the chair is made to support the weight of the person sitting on it. I also find that when I am engaged in art, writing ideas come to me, for often good story ideas are not so much pursued as received when your mind is in a receptive state.

6. Keep a notebook you may call a journal, a log, or something else.

When I called my notebook a journal, it evoked pretentious literary generalizations that embarrassed me. Now I call the notebook a daybook, and it has become a sort of traveling office in which I can scribble ideas, draft leads, brainstorm, map, record overheard conversations, list unexpected statistics, diagram pieces of writing, write drafts, and carry on a continuous conversation with myself about my work, how it is going, how it isn't going, and where it should go.

That notebook is with me all the time. It is the place where I work during those fragments of time that are often wasted. In it I write sitting in the doctor's waiting room, during the traffic jam, while the commercials interrupt the ballgame, or when I'm waiting for the meeting to start. I prefer a spiral notebook that prevents gaps in the continuing chronological record of what I am doing and what I may do next. I keep a small tape recorder with me when I'm driving and make oral notes that I transfer to the daybook later. Starting a new notebook, about every two months, I go through the one just finished and list ideas that still interest me in the beginning of the notebook.

7. Compost. Keep a file drawer of reports, brochures, handouts, speeches, magazine articles, newspaper clippings, photos, letters, drafts that didn't work—all sorts of stuff. Go through the file every few months and turn it over the way you would a compost pile; see what connects. Throw most of it away, but you'll also unearth material that you've been collecting on topics that can make good stories.

8. Role-play. Make believe you are the prisoner or the person being arrested, the lobbyist or the legislator, the judge or the member of the jury, the waiter or the cook, the factory worker or the labor leader, the twenty-year-old without an education or the thirty-year-old with too much education. Journalists are frighteningly similar in educational background and economic position. They are predominantly white, college-educated, living in the suburbs or the chic inner city, members of the professional class. Journalists don't like that picture of themselves. They imagine that they are rebels, but in this country they are very tame rebels, insiders in society, members of the five percent or fewer who imagine that they run things.

If that's who we are, it is our obligation to at least use our imagination to extend the limits of our world. Role-playing is one way we can step out of the usual costumes and experience other lives so that we will know the questions to ask to get a fully documented story.

9. Buy a different magazine each week. Buy a science magazine, such as *Discover,* this week; a literary magazine, such as the *Massachusetts Review,* next week. Try *Trailer Life, Backpacker, Money, Fortune, Mother Jones.* Almost every interest—or perversion—has its own publication. Read them, the ads as well as the text. Tear out the most interesting articles and carry a small file of those to read in spare moments so that you can extend your world.

10. When you are on a story look for the authorities other people turn to and interview them. In the accident ward you will notice doctors deferring to one nurse; at the garage one mechanic is called over for an expert diagnosis; at the fire one fireman is consulted to decide if the roof is safe; at the Senate hearings the "names" will look at a staff member for direction. Newspapers will have better stories if we discover these hidden authorities and interview them.

11. The poet sees poems, the novelist novels, the dramatist plays. A good way to get new ideas is to look at the world through the lens of another form of writing. If you've been writing profiles it may be good for you to write a straight news account or an editorial about something in your territory. If you've been writing editorials it may be a good idea to go out and do a profile. You may want to imagine your beat being covered by a screenwriter, a historian, a mystery writer, a *New Yorker* profile writer. Write a few pages in this new genre using the approach and the language to help you see the familiar anew. A few of these pieces may be publishable, but that's not their purpose. They help you use your craft to see the stories under your pen that you should cover.

12. Sit in one place for an hour and make notes of what you see: what people are wearing, how they move, how they treat each other, the message their behavior sends and returns, details that reveal the mood of the place, differences you might have seen ten or twenty years ago, differences you may see ten or twenty years from now, things that surprise you, the most important thing you are seeing. We are, after all, reporters, but we usually go out to report only what we—or our editors—expect to see.

13. Always have at least one book in the briefcase or on the bed table outside your everyday interests. Some suggestions:

PriaryErth
William Least Heat-Moon (Houghton Mifflin, 1991).

What Work Is
Phillip Levine (Knopf, 1991).

Remembering the Bone House
Nancy Mairs (Harper & Row, 1989; Perennial Library, 1990).

Notbooks of the Mind
Vera John-Steiner (University of New Mexico Press, 1985).

Wartime
Paul Fussell (Oxford University Press, 1989).

You Just Don't Understand
Deborah Tannen (William Morrow, 1990).

A Midwife's Tale
Laurel Thatcher Ulrich (Knopf, 1990).

A Natural History of the Senses
Diane Ackerman (Random House, 1990; Vintage, 1991).

Any book of poetry by Charles Simic (Braziller, et al) or Mekeel
McBride (Carnegie-Mellon).

Amoskeag: Life and Work in an American Factory City
Tamara K. Hareven and Randolph Langenbach (Pantheon, 1978).

Photography and the Art of Seeing
Freeman Patterson (Van Nostrand Reinhold, 1979).

The Bluest Eye
Toni Morrison (Washington Square Press).

A Writer's Diary
Virginia Woolf (Harcourt Brace, 1973; Signet).

Mechanics of the Mind
Colin Blakemore (Cambridge University Press, 1977).

Experimental Drawing
Robert Kaupelis (Watson Guptill, 1980).

Thirty Seconds
Michael J. Arlen (Farrar, Straus, 1980; Penguin).

Reporting
Lillian Ross (Simon & Schuster, 1964; Touchstone).

Tides and the Pull of the Moon
Francis E. Wylie (Stephen Greene Press, 1974).

14. Free write. Sit down and write as fast as you can for a few minutes. It is amazing how much you can write in four-, six-, ten-, fifteen-minute writing periods. Let the language lead you toward meaning. If you free write frequently you will be surprised how many ideas will come from these unplanned pages.

• • •

I'm always shocked to see bored people in a city room. You expect bored people in post offices, legislatures, and on college campuses. The one thing that comforts me most, traveling far into terminal middle age, is that I shall never write all the stories I have to write. There will always be new ideas, forms I haven't yet attempted, voices I haven't mastered. Every morning at my desk I will find new and interesting ways to fail.

As reporters we are given license to pry, to be nosy, to be forever curious, to learn. Insatiable curiosity is the quality common to the famous editors I have known. When you first met him Henry Luce, a found of Time, *was like a terrier with his questions. So too was DeWitt Wallace, who created* Reader's Digest. *An editor who has this quality is Tom Winship. I was on a trip to Alaska with him and he was always at the people he met to tell him more, always excited by what he learned about oil wells, seals, ice, people. Once he heard me speak, and afterward he wanted to see my notes, how I made them, how they were covered in plastic, the kind of notebook I used. His hunger for detail was never satisfied.*

I can hear the garumphs and harumphs from the old sea lions who inhabit the city room; "So what if I have great ideas. The Globe doesn't want 'em." That depends. Some editors do encourage ideas from their staff, and some do not. But I think every writer can devise a strategy to deal with the problem. Here's the one I followed at the Boston Herald.

- *I'm in charge of my own career. It is my responsibility—and in my selfish best interest—to come in with story ideas I want to pursue.*

- *Editors can't see the ideas in my head. Therefore: If the story depends on a concept, I give the editor a brief outline. I draft the lead I hope I will be able to write, list the major points (no more than five), point out why the story should be written, how the information will be gathered, and how much time and space it will take. If the story depends on tone—if it is a mood piece or humor—I write a draft and show it to the editor.*

- *I expect rejections. Editors are hard to educate, but the more ideas I have, the more ideas I will have. And if the idea is really good and the paper I'm working for has been given a fair opportunity to see its importance and is not interested, then I query a magazine or book publisher and write the story on my own time. The paper needs your ideas, but even more than that you need to be having ideas so that you are not bored and are alive, aware of the world in which you live.*

SEVEN

AVOIDING THE CLICHES OF VISION

The more professional we become the greater the danger that we will see what we expect to see. Experience, of course, is an advantage, but it has a dark side. It may keep us from seeing the real story: the cause that does not fit the stereotype, the effect that is not predictable, the quote that we do not hear before our question is answered. The effective writer must always have an essential naiveté; skepticism must be balanced by innocence. The reporter must be capable of seeing what is new.

Clichés of language are significant misdemeanors, but clichés of vision are felonies. Too often editors punish each misdemeanor but advocate the commission of felonies.

A young man has run amok in the neighborhood, killing eight and maiming fifteen. The man is described as quiet, studious, polite to the neighbors, good to his mother, neat, mild-mannered, and the last person in the world you would have expected to do anything like that. Carol McCabe tells about the mother of one such young man, who said, "He never did anything like that before." He is the cliché killer, and the reporter is happy to find him. There's no problem writing the story; it's been written before, and before, and before. The neighbors all fall into the stereotype. They aren't lying, but they are shocked; they do like the mother; they want to avoid responsibility for what they've overlooked the last twenty years. And besides, they know the journalistic stereotypes as well as the reporters do.

Some good, hard-edged reporting will discover that neighborhood pets have been disappearing for years, the nice young man was seen cooking pigeons when he was three years old; that he didn't play doctor but Nazi torturer; that the neighbors have called the police eleven times for acts of violence against his mother; that his father, two brothers, and three sisters have refused to live at home with him; that the studious young man has the reading level of a nine-year-old; and that his mother has fought a guerrilla war against getting psychiatric help for him since he was three years old.

And that story may lead to other stories: Poor kids get better counseling help than middle-class kids; early help for disturbed children is crucial; nearby agencies provide such help; there are danger signals that neighbors and teachers should pay attention to.

In journalism we too often leave the city room knowing what we'll find, and then, of course, we find it. This cliché is compounded by editors who tell reporters what to find and give them a hard time when they don't fill in the blanks of the editor's stereotype.

Some of the stereotypes of vision are:

- The victim is always innocent.
- Corporation executives are workaholics.
- Bureaucrats are lazy.
- Housewives hate being housewives.
- Politicians are crooked.
- All gays cruise.
- It's lonely at the top.
- It's boring in the suburbs.
- It's exciting in the city.
- There's never a peaceful evening on a Roxbury street corner

where good friends spend a few peaceful hours reminiscing and kidding each other; there's never a Friday evening in a New Hampshire country store marked by distrust, meanness, and potential violence.

You could count 11,721 journalistic stereotypes. We know them all, and our readers do too. That may be one reason some papers have fewer readers.

The old rewrite man, wearing an eyeshade because his whiskey eyes couldn't stand light, would write a newspaper in an hour before deadline. He (and Alice Burke of the old *Boston Traveler*) wrote the same stories day after day. I admired these old mythmakers, learned from them, and was proud to discover that I could work rewrite myself. But today's rewrite persons are over at channels 4, 5, and 7, cutting film into clichés measured by seconds, and the newspaper has the opportunity to go beyond the stereotypes.

The reporter has the challenge of getting the unexpected material into the notebook that will become a story with density, feeling, a point of view, and voice.

Here are reminders of what goes into the good reporter's notebook:

1. What isn't being said—significant pauses, distances, facial expressions, gestures, body actions and reactions.

2. The details of the environment that the news sources create. The gadgets on the desk, the books on the shelf, the pictures on the wall are usually calculated to reveal, but the person they reveal, sometimes, is not what they expect. Once I interviewed the leader of an organization working to control the birth rate around the world. His own desk was crowded with pictures of his large family. His double-standard answers were revealing in a way he did not intend.

3. Listen to what you're hearing, not what you expect to hear. On one story I found that a grandmother who took in a grandson and did a marvelous job of raising him was motivated not by grandmother love but by mother-in-law hatred. It was a stronger and a truer story.

4. Put the reader on the scene. A hearing isn't just testimony; it involves people, place, action, and reaction.

5. Don't just talk to members of Kiwanis. Many newspapers read as if their communities were composed entirely of lawyers, opticians, and realtors, who spend most of their time giving each other plaques. Make sure you talk to the old and the young, the housewife as well as the career woman, the building inspector as well as the mayor, the factory worker as well as the factory owner, the fireman as well as the policeman, the nonunion worker as well as the union member, the quiet as well as the loud, the contented as well as the discontented.

6. Look for stories that have no event. Many of the most significant developments in our society never come to trial and are never the subject of a press conference on television. Some stories that should be covered: The 100,000-mile cars that are repainted instead of being turned in, the shirt collars that re being turned, the thirty-five-year-old children who are still living at home, he additions that are being built on houses because people can't afford larger homes, the huge increase in home vegetable gardens, the increase in women sewing and tailoring for men as well as women, and sewing done by men.

7. Practice empathetic reporting. Get inside the skin of the judge on the bench, the prosecutor, the defender, the witness, the victim, the criminal, the parent, the wife, the child. Become each person for a moment so that you will know the questions to ask that reveal the point of view and the attitude of each participant.

Make your own list of the ways in which you can see the stories that aren't appearing in the daily paper—and should.

EIGHT

WHAT TO DO WHEN YOU HAVE TO WRITE THE SAME STORY AGAIN AND AGAIN AND . . .

Looking back I realized I played an important writing game when I served time on rewrite on the old *Boston Herald,* zipping out twenty, thirty, forty stories a night.

The game is simple: How can I do something different that will be true to the story and work within the limitations of space and deadline?

This game is one of the reasons that at sixty-seven I am eager to write another column, draft another revision of one of my books, work over a poem, or return to the novel. I may say the same old thing but I keep finding new ways of approaching the old subjects because of the game.

I do not, of course, play the game on every story, but I play it when there is a hint of repetition or a too-comfortable familiarity as I start to work. The new ways of saying the old thing do not have to be large to satisfy me—my standards are low—but they have to give me a problem to solve.

Mihaly Csikszentmihalyi and Jacob W. Getzels wrote a book, *The Creative Vision,* that is on the shelf across from my desk because it reports on a long-term study of artists documenting that the successful ones find problems to solve where others see no problems—a good lesson for all of us.

All stories, even those in the Bible, are old stories. But there are ways that we can make them new, for the moment, both for our readers and for ourselves. There are three particular areas where we can seek new challenges, new ways to tell old stories. We are not, of course, discovering a new planet, but we are assigning ourselves explorations of our craft that will make our work more interesting to ourselves and our readers.

Old Stories Seen in New Ways

Each story can be seen in many ways. Here are a few that may expose a new story within an old one:

- Change the angle of vision from the senator to the senator's aide, the view of the opponent, the voter, the lobbyist, the citizen affected by the vote. Most stories are told from a predictable angle of vision. Move the angle of vision just a bit and you may see a new story in an old one, a story that reveals the essence of the story more effectively.

- Focus on a single person: the criminal, the victim, the arresting officer, that officer's partner, a senior officer, a rookie, a member of the victim's family, the criminal's family, the officer's family, the DA, the police photographer, the ambulance driver, the trauma doctor, the trauma nurse. Go on. There may be a hundred different ways a single event is seen. Choose the most significant, not the most traditional, one.

- Put the story in a historical perspective.

- Put the story in context. Show how it relates, how it influences and is influenced by the world around it.

- Look ahead and see what may happen because of the event.

- Describe the process of the story in detail, not, for a change, yanking the events out of sequence to order them for the reader, but showing how the event evolved.

- Focus on the background instead of the foreground—the technology available, considered, rejected, and used in the trauma center.

- Focus on the conflict behind the scenes that caused the conflict within the story.

- Take the reader into the committee room, the police dispatch center, or the company sales meeting so the reader is within the event taking place.

Old Stories in a New Form

There are a limited number of forms in traditional journalism and we keep distorting the news (and boring our readers) by shoehorning all stories into those forms. Worse still, most of us use only one, two, or three of those forms to tell all our stories. We do what we are comfortable doing and that's what is often wrong with stories: they are comfortable, familiar, ho-hummers.

- Tell the story as a story. Use narrative to reveal the beginning, middle, and end of the conflict ordered by time.
- Write the event through a profile.
- Tell it with an interview with one person or several.
- Create a dialogue between contestants. Let them reveal the story.
- Reveal by a scene: characters, action (usually dialogue), conflict and resolution, setting.
- Write it as a rhetorical form central to the story: a police report, a political speech, a company memo, a nursing report, a job application, a letter by a participant to a friend.
- Film the story in print, moving the camera in close and back, to reveal it to the reader in images and scenes.
- Use lists, parallel columns, charts, or other devices appropriate to the story to reveal its significance clearly to the reader.
- Select the central scene, conflict, personality, or issue in the story and write a forty-line story focussing in on it.

Old Stories Told in a New Voice

The voice (the style, the tone, the music) of the story provides an opportunity to make familiar (dull?) stories lively and more effective. The tuning of the writer's voice to the message of the story is also a game of craft that can be satisfying to the writer and increase the writer's involvement in stories that have been written repeatedly.

- Look for the phrase that reveals the central issue of the story: Tom Palmer's use of "We want to stay" in an East German protest story; Brian Mooney's lead, "Dapper O'Neil was at home among strangers . . ."
- Match the tone of the story to the meaning of the story: controlled

anger, nostalgia, humor, cynicism, historical recollection, grief, wonder.

- Use the tone of the people in the story—angry workers, fire victims, pols, police, intellectuals, commuters, business consultants, doctors, lawyers.

- Throw a change of pace. Relieve the pressure on the reader with a touch of humor in a serious piece, a touch of seriousness in a humorous piece, an anecdote in a solemn report, or a bit of old-fashioned solemnity in a lively, anecdotal yarn.

- Vary the documentation. Use what will help the reader, not what you are used to using in a particular story. Stories shouldn't be limited to one traditional form of documentation such as anecdotes, quotes, or statistics.

- Vary the length of sentences and paragraphs. Use shorter ones for the most important points.

- Set goals for your own writing. Decide you are going to work on one thing this month: writing shorts, trying humor, making people alive on the page, learning to use more statistics more effectively.

- Write aloud and read aloud, using the sound of the words and sentences (the beat, the pace, the rhythm) to reinforce the meaning of the story.

- Focus on one section of the writing this week, another next week: endings, leads, turning points, description, and so on.

- Take the clichés of our business and put a twist on them: local businessmen/local and almost-local businesspersons; Beacon Hill pols/Beacon Hill reps, elected and self-elected; housewives/home managers. None of these are great and yours probably won't be either, but they are fun to write and read. Bad as they may be, they aren't as bad as what we use without thinking.

- Stir in a bit of surprise. Use the unexpected word, phrase, line, or tone when it does a more effective job of revealing the story.

Be selfish. Take command of your own stories. Make them fun. Risk. Try what you don't think you can do. Teach yourself in print. On each story set up a new challenge. Our craft is, after all, based on play, and we must never take it so seriously that we forget to play with what we see, how we order it, and how we tell it to ourselves and our readers.

NINE

Interview:
KEVIN CULLEN

Globe writers and editors repeatedly express their respect for the traditional skills displayed by Kevin Cullen as he produces hard news stories on deadline that have his own special touch. He rarely has the time for the long takeout but works within precise limitations of time and space. He is a master of selection.

How do you spot and cultivate a good source?

Spotting a good source is being able to see through the trees and recognize the person most capable in any given field. In law enforcement, or any form of government, for that matter, it is seldom the person of highest rank.

There's no easy way to recognize these people, except to listen to what people say. Who's respected, and who's considered a bozo by the vast majority. You have to follow your instincts.

Keeping a source is easy. Once you get him or her talking you've got to show results. You've got to get stories in the paper. And, despite the urge to tilt things the source's way, you've got to resist and play it as fairly as possible.

How do you get people to talk and capture the way they speak?

When I interview a longshoreman, my Boston accent is much thicker. *I pahk my cah and tawk to da guy.* When I interview criminals, I swear a lot, because they swear a lot. When I talk to priests, my parochial school deference comes through. *Fahtha this and Fahtha that.* When I talk to lawyers, I use as much legal jargon as possible, to demonstrate I'm not the usual dolt layperson. When I talk to old ladies in South Boston, I'm polite. When I talk to a cop whose partner has been gunned down in front of him, I'm sympathetic. A reporter shouldn't be an actor, but creating an atmosphere in which the interview subject is most natural and comfortable usually cuts through the crap and gets the subject talking freely.

How do you take notes?

Not nearly as well as I should. I find it hard not to look at the person I'm talking to, and I find it hard to look at them and take legible, good notes. A tape recorder is a pain, except if you have the luxury of time. Besides, a recorder can sometimes make people ill at ease and kill that free exchange you're trying to promote.

The most important thing to do is to guard against stopping an interview simply because you think you've got all you need for a forty- or sixty-line story. I find some of the best quotes come out much later in the interview, which stands to reason, because that is usually when the person loosens up and some kind of rapport has developed between interviewer and interviewee.

How do you make use of notes?

The most essential thing is to read them. Very often, I find if I don't read my notes over carefully, I'll miss a key quote or piece of color, simply because I've forgotten that came up in the interview.

What do you try to do in a lead?

A hard news lead should be as short as possible. This is Journalism School 101 stuff. I think it's pretty hard to explain anything to anyone at our level about writing a hard news lead. You either hit the right things or you don't.

The softer lead is a different matter, much more subjective. My own feeling is that, whenever you have the material to support it, a soft lead can be used to lure in more readers than a hard news lead ever could.

A soft lead, which is a misnomer if it is done well, should be striking. It should make people read a line and say, "Hmm, this looks interesting. That sounds wild." It should read like the first line of a Frank O'Connor short story: striking for its simplicity, but immediately conveying the reader that the author knows his stuff. The lead should carry the confidence of the author.

I think leads should set the tone for the rest of the story. If it's a bizarre story, use a bizarre lead; if a sad story, a sad lead; if funny, funny.

What process do you use going through the draft?

I don't use outlines. I write stream of (somewhat) consciousness. I usually try to get the lead down first. If the kicker is the next to come to mind, that goes down at the bottom. If a nice transition pops into my head, even if it will eventually find its way to the next-to-last paragraph, that goes down. The key is to keep writing, keep the juices flowing. My biggest problem is getting side-tracked—getting phone calls or working on something else even while I'm writing.

How do you hear and tune a strong voice?

You listen. If you listen, you hear. Don't be afraid to include a "Jesus Christ" or an "I mean" if they say it, as that's how may people begin their sentences in conversation. That creates a strong, credible voice.

How do you get a strong sense of the people you're reporting on and the places where they live and work into your notebook and your stories?

Being from the Boston area, I have a lifelong knowledge of the area that cannot be replaced by books or anything short of total immersion, like a Tony Lukas in *Common Ground,* but who has the time for that?

When I went to Northern Ireland on assignment, I drew on past experience, including living in Dublin for a year and in Belfast for several months. I also drew on past reading. But, remembering all that, I listened to what people said and tried to report that faithfully. No big secret.

How do you pace your stories?

As I mentioned before, I think, except for a straight, hard news story, they should read like short stories. There should be a beginning, a middle, and an end, with catchy, well-turned transitions in between. Quotes are great transitional vehicles. Mechanically speaking, it's good to remember that a long sentence should be followed by a short one or two. That creates a pace for the reader.

Problems?

My stories are late too often. Sometimes it's because I dwell on transitions and things like that too much. Often it's because I try to make too many phone calls late in the afternoon.

That problem seems to be getting worse, not better, as I get older and become more conscious of the importance of writing. My previous tabloid mentality was: Screw it, if you have it first, you did your job, the hell with presentation. Now I want to have it first but write it well. Hopefully, it will solve itself as I become more confident in my own ability. There's a mental roadblock in that. I feel if I put less time into my work down the road, I'm not doing as thorough a job.

Do you have any writers whom you use as models or guides? Any books you would suggest other reporters read?

Probably the greatest influence on me has been the work of Frank O'Connor, the Irish short-story writer. I admired Ray Fitzgerald, the late *Globe* sportswriter, growing up, and I always thought that Mike Barnicle could tell a story because he knows how people, all people, feel.

I would recommend that anyone interested in writing better news stories under deadline pressure read O'Connor's collected works, which I stole from Diana Altera two years ago and haven't returned.

TEN

Interview:
STEVE KURKJIAN

One of the most significant developments in contemporary journalism is the institutionalizing of investigative teams that have special financial support, extensive time and resources, independence from daily news operation, and particular skills.

The *Globe* Spotlight Team won the Pulitzer Prize in 1972 and 1980, the Sigma Delta Chi Public Service Award in 1972, the Associated Press Managing Editors' Award in 1977, the Headliners Award for Outstanding Public Service in 1978, the Associated Press Sevellon Brown Award in 1979 and 1980, the National Consumer Foundation Award in 1975, and the New England United Press International Community Service Award in 1972, 1978, 1979, and 1980.

Steve Kurkjian, news projects editor of the *Globe,* was an original member of the paper's investigative unit, the Spotlight Team, and was head of the team at the time of the interview. He is known at the *Globe* for his ability to get people to talk who do not want to talk.

How do you prepare for an interview?

People dread being mentioned in any investigative article, even if they are not the main focus of the story, and so it's no wonder that their first reaction on getting a call from a Spotlight reporter is to refuse an interview. No set formula works in dealing with a reluctant interviewee. But before every interview I prepare a long list, a short list, and a "hello-goodbye" list of questions I will use depending on the person's reaction to my call.

How do you start the interview?

The most crucial time is the first two minutes, during which you don't let the subject do too much talking because his first reaction is going to be negative. The things I try to impress on him during that period are written into my "patter." They include:

1. I already know most of what went on from other people I've interviewed.

2. Some of the people I've interviewed have mentioned his name as a person who could add one or two things and whose word can be trusted.

3. It is very important that I speak to as many people as possible because this is a vital story, with all sorts of social and political consequences, and I have to be absolutely sure of my facts. (This plays to his conscience—if he doesn't talk, then he is conspiring in the printing of a story that may be inaccurate.)

4. I am a good guy, who has worked like hell on this story; he is a good guy for not having gotten too deeply involved in the skulduggery; and we have a common body of interests and are really working the same side of the road.

Even if the person is the one and only source who can provide the whole story, I don't let him think the entire article rests with him. It's too heavy a load for one person to bear to think that it's his word against someone else's. Few people want to become martyrs, and those who do have usually lost their perspective and objectivity and so aren't much help.

What do you do after the "patter" stage?

The best way to proceed is to go for those one or two nuggets of information that you want this person to confirm, deny, or elaborate on right after you have finished your patter. If he's expansive after that, ask him to "step back" a little and go for more cosmic information, such as, "How could this have happened?" or "Why didn't official investigative bodies stop this right away?" If he opens up here all of a sudden, he's the expert and is leading you through the rocks and shoals of a complicated story. Foster that feeling in him, even if it's stuff you already know about.

Are there hazards in this approach?

The only problem with such an approach is that the source begins to feel superior in his relationship with you, which means he feels he could lie to you about something to make himself look good. The best way of dealing with that, I've found, is to impress on him that you need accurate information all the way through; that if one middle initial is out of place, the whole story could be rebutted. If you find he continues to lie or exaggerate facts, confront him with it in a direct manner. But don't be offensive, because he could always hang up leaving you with nothing.

What conditions do you prefer for an interview?

I like to call at the home of a background source I need to give me the substance of my story. He feels more comfortable at home, less a part of the corporate or government structure on which you are asking him to give damaging information. I tell him that I'm calling from my home, giving him the impression I am so thoroughly committed to the story that I will work day and night for it. If he gets a positive feeling about the person he is speaking with, he is more apt to talk and talk honestly.

Interview the principal of the story in his office. Ask to tape record the interview. It saves you from taking notes and mistaking a quote. If he's hesitant, we offer to provide him with a copy of the transcript of the interview.

What standards do you have for confirming information?

I do not like to take anyone's word for anything unless I have a document supporting the contentions. Of course, we don't always have the time or the ability to get the documentation even if it exists. I've adopted an informal guide that I will not float an allegation of illegality against anyone unless hard documentation is in hand, or there are several supporting sources. I think it is wrong to hold a reporter to the standard of getting three confirming sources before publishing a story; some allegations should require half a dozen such sources, others just two.

Rehearse:
Write Before Writing

When I study my own writing process and the writing process of other experienced writers, I discover that 60 to 80 percent of the writing process is completed before the first draft. Inversely, most reporters who have difficulty writing try to begin their writing process with the first draft, coming to the desk with little idea of how they may begin.

As a full-time writer I try to get in two to three hours of writing between 7:30 and 11:30 in the morning, but most of the writing is actually done between 11:30 one morning and 7:30 the next morning. Experienced writers rehearse what they may say, turning over the specific information from which an effective story may be built, connecting that information in many patterns of potential meaning, listening for the voice of what they may write.

It may not be easy to live with a writer who is, at best, present half of the time. As James Thurber reported, "I never quite know when I'm writing. Sometimes my wife comes up to me at a party and says, 'Damnit, Thurber, stop writing.' She usually catches me in the middle of a paragraph." The process of rehearsal is essential to a writer.

Rehearsal occurs in many places besides parties. It may take place in the cavern of the brain, during subconscious and unconscious thought, in night dreaming and daydreaming. Or, as Paul Theroux says, "Many writers I have known talk to themselves. I have this mumbling habit; it has served me well . . . as an imaginative rehearsal for writing." Rehearsal may also occur in the writing to myself that I do in my daybook, which is always with me, or in the laptop computer I keep by my living room chair or carry with me as I fly across the U.S. or to other countries.

During rehearsal the writing ripens. Virginia Woolf once wrote, "As for my next book, I am going to hold myself from writing it till I have it impending in me: grown heavy in my mind like a ripe pear; pendant, gravid, asking to be cut or it will fall." The writer comes to the desk with the draft already begun.

ELEVEN

LEADING WITH THE LEAD

Readers make the decision to read or not to read after a sentence, two sentences, a paragraph, or two paragraphs. It's all over in a matter of seconds.

Listen to what the masters, and mistresses, of our craft say about the importance of the lead to the writer:

Raymond Carver:

I have that opening line and then everything seems to radiate out from that line.

Joan Didion:

What's so hard about the first sentence is that you're stuck with it. Everything else is going to flow out of that sentence. And by the time you've laid down the first TWO sentences, your options are all gone.

Paul Horgan:

The most important sentence in a good book is the first one: it will contain the organic seed from which all that follows will grow.

Elie Wiesel

The first line sets the tone, the melody. If I hear the tone, the melody, then I have the book.

And yet the beginnings—the first few lines that will capture or turn off a reader—in most newspapers are poorly written and poorly read. Readers move to other stories or to radio and television.

Some of the most common problems with news leads are:

Cluttered. The reader has no time to breathe. They read as "save-my-ass" leads: No editor can say the writer left anything out. Leads can be one sentence long. Some material can be put in the second paragraph or even the third.

Flabby. I don't know what the story is about and if the writer is this confused, I don't care.

Dull. Ho-hum. There is no tension, no energy that drives the writing forward. If the writer is bored . . .

Mechanical. There is no human voice, no music, just another hamburger.

Closed. This is private conversation between people who speak the same jargon. Stay away, you don't know enough to read this story.

Predictable. I know what will be said and how it will be said. It is written in journalese, the words and phrases that are the clichés of our craft. There are no surprises of language, no words and phrases that are unexpected and delight us as they capture and clarify a news event.

How the Lead Serves the Reader

An effective lead makes a promise to the reader. If the lead promises information the reader needs or wants, the reader continues. If the promise is attractive, readers who do not know they want or need the information continue.

Readers are in a hurry and have many distractions, and we have seconds—no more—in which to catch and hold the reader's attention. Readers are selfish. They flip through the paper asking: "What's in this story for me?"; "Why should I read about another housing scandal?"

We have to say what's in the story for them, why they should read this story, and do it in a line, three lines, or five at the most. And those aren't the lines you are typing on the screen. They are column lines. We should tell ourselves that we have half a line on the screen, a line and a half, or two and a half lines to capture the reader, no more.

The lead promises specific, accurate information the reader wants or needs. The good lead entices; it promises clarity, grace, and delight— something more than the reader expects. The lead promises to satisfy the reader's expectations: A news story delivers something new, a profile reveals a person, a narrative tells a story, an exposé exposes, an analysis goes below the surface. The lead provides a tension that produces the energy that drives the story forward. And the lead promises a closing, a sense of completion by the last lines of the article.

The writer must be aware of the promises made in the lead if they are to be fulfilled. And therein lies the importance of the lead for the writer.

How the Lead Serves the Writer

The lead tells the writer how to write the story. It focuses, orders, shapes the message, and establishes the story's voice. An effective lead solves most of the problems the writer will face in the first draft and solves them efficiently, ahead of time, when the writer is not trapped in a tangle of prose.

Let's examine the problems that can be solved by the lead:

Focus. The lead establishes the central tension of the story. Everything in the story will support and advance the significance of that tension.

Context. The lead places the central tension of the story in context. The story exists in a particular world that has its own history, its possible futures, and its relationship to the reader.

Form. In the first lines the reader, and therefore the writer, is told what the form of the story will be: narrative, profile, exposé, backgrounder, feature, news event, etcetera.

Evidence. The effective lead often provides a sample of the type of evidence on which the story rests (statistics, quotations, observation, anecdote, and so on) and implies the abundance of the evidence that will be delivered to the reader.

Voice. Each text has its own voice, the voice of the writer tuned to the material. That heard quality in the story plays as important—perhaps even more important—a role as background music in a movie. The voice of the story is established in the first line, often in the first few words. The voice supports the material, tells the reader the significance of the material, instructs the reader how to respond to the story, and becomes the human element in the story, creating a compelling personal conversation between writer and individual reader.

Authority. Must be established in the lead if the reader is to believe the information in the article and respect its significance.

Audience. Each effective story is targeted for a specific reader in the lead.

Length. The lead implies the length of the story: a news bulletin, a takeout, a reconstruction, a single interview, or a roundup.

Pace. The lead establishes the pace at which the story is to be written, whether the story is a quick, hard-hitting series of actions and reactions; a leisurely walk-through; a street-corner, on-the-scene interview; or a reflective conversation about a past event.

Order. The lead often predicts the order of the story: chronological, inverted pyramid, or cause and effect.

End. The lead usually implies the nature of the ending, since the last few lines may echo the lead in content or style, may answer the question raised in the lead, or may reveal a situation set up by the lead but now more clearly understood because of the information in the story.

Complicated? Darn right. But time spent on the lead is worthwhile because it controls and predicts everything that follows.

How Lead Writing Speeds Up Writing

The secret to productivity is the lead. It would appear that careful attention to writing and rewriting leads would result in writers who stay in the batter's box and never march up to the plate. That can happen, but most of us who write fast do so because we concentrate on getting the lead right before we move on. Each lead I draft in my head and on the screen is a mini-draft of the entire piece; the lead allows me to see problems ahead and to avoid or solve them before they bog down the draft.

Because of a trip to Europe followed by illness and a death in the family, I was jammed up to deadline a few years ago. I had to write half of a new edition of a book in one week. I wrote 235 pages in seven days, an average of 33½ pages a day, 20 of them new, the rest revised. How did I do it? By getting the lead to each chapter and to each section right and then writing fast, the way everyone on a newspaper should be able to write.

When I started to sell magazine articles, I had to learn to write leads. I was a first-draft, newspaper lead writer. I could spot a stock (cliché) lead on the shelf as well as anyone, grab it, and use it. Magazines wanted more, and for years I drafted fifty to seventy-five leads for every story. I don't keep score anymore and I suspect that after fifty years of writing, I don't write that many leads; but I draft them in my head, scribble them down in my daybook, and draft them on the screen.

And the closer the deadline, the more time I spend on the lead. Not hours, but minutes. It takes a couple of minutes, one minute, seconds even to draft a possible first line. Five, ten, fifteen first lines, each with a different approach, and I find myself homing in on one. It is more a matter of this is right, this will work, than these are wrong, those will not work. I do more first lines, perhaps first paragraphs, polishing, fitting, and shaping, and I am off.

When I am lucky that process takes place during the reporting and thinking stages of writing. It is a matter of five minutes here, three minutes there while I am waiting to see someone, driving the car, watching television, taking my morning walk, sitting in a parking lot, reading, or even writing another article or chapter. When I am on deadline, it is a matter of doing that in the first fifteen minutes, give or take five minutes, of the writing.

Qualities of an Effective Lead

The leads that attract readers and lure them into reading the story usually have similar qualities.

Focus. The lead makes a specific promise to the reader. That promise is contained in a tension that will be released and resolved by the reading of the story.

Context. The promise of the lead exists in a world that involves the reader. It has clear, immediate significance for the reader.

Form. The lead implies a form (design, structure, pattern) that will help the reader understand the meaning of the information in the story.

Information. Statistics, quotations, revealing details, and description whet the reader's hunger for information and promise it will be satisfied in the story.

Voice. This is an individual human voice tuned to the purpose of the story, a voice that provides the music to support the meaning of what is being read.

Surprise. The promise of something new, something that will give the reader the opportunity to become an authority on the subject and surprise those with whom the reader works and lives.

Forms of Effective Leads

Take a piece of paper and list the leads you have in your toolbox. Most of us have many more ways of beginning a piece of writing than we realize. And writing such a list reminds us of leads we have read and those we might invent. Some of the leads in my toolbox are:

News. Tells the reader what the reader needs to know in the order the reader needs to know it. Who, what, when, where, why.

Anecdote. A brief story that reveals the essence of your subject.

Quotation. A quote lead can give additional authority and a fresh voice to a story.

Umbrella. Covers several equal elements in the story.

Descriptive. Sets the scene for the story.

Voice. Voice establishes the tone of the story.

Announcement. Tells the reader what you are going to say.

Tension. Reveals the forces in the story and sets them in motion.

Problem. Establishes the problem that will be solved in the article.

Background. Provides the background so that the reader will understand the importance of the story.

Historical. Places the story in a historical context.

Narrative. Establishes the story as the form of the article.

Question. Involves the reader in the fundamental issue of the story.

Point of View. Establishes the position from which the reader will be shown the subject.

Reader Identification. Shows readers how the story relates to them.

Face. Gives the reader a person with whom to identify during the reading of the story.

Scene. Sets up an action between participants in the story that reveals the central meaning of the article.

Dialogue. Allows the story's meaning to come from the interaction of principal people in the story.

Process. Involves the reader in a process central to the meaning of the story.

These are only a few of the ways to write leads. Each has advantages and disadvantages. The anecdote or quote lead may pull the reader away from the true focus of the story; the backgrounder may delay the real beginning so long the reader will move to another story; the question lead will be patronizing—"We do want to take our shot, don't we?"; but we should look to see what lead will best reveal each story and attract readers to that story.

Thirty Questions to Produce Effective Leads

The more experienced the writer, the more the writer delights in discovering new ways to find the lead. Sometimes writers turn to editors or colleagues and tell them the story so that they can "hear" the lead the writer has not seen. At other times writers make outlines or diagrams to see the focal point—a potential lead. Some writers find it helpful to look back at a collection of good leads they've saved.

Look around the city room and you will see writers waiting for the gift of a good lead from the muse. Some writers hope to find the lead in a coffee cup, others in bummed cigarettes. Some keep looking for the lead in the rest room, others in the cafeteria. All writers know that good leads come through the window, and so writers stare out of windows. But because only *Globe* editors have windows, *Globe* writers stare past the empty expression on the faces of other lead-searchers staring past them.

If staring out of imaginary windows, sipping stale coffee, and meditating on the can doesn't work, however, here is an emergency checklist of thirty questions desperate lead-hunters may ask themselves.

1. What one thing does the reader need to know more than any other?

The most common problem, even for experienced writers, is focus. The story simply does not have one dominant point, but in almost any story one issue, situation, or action should dominate. Step back and think a minute, limit yourself to one quick note, and you may come up with "rule vote," "inquest set," or "effect on patients." Such a code phrase may help you to see where to start building a lead.

If one thing doesn't come to mind, it may help to list the three, four, or five most important elements in the story, and then number them in the order of their importance. When the story is stripped down to its basics you can usually see what is most important.

2. What would make the reader turn and say, "Now listen to this, Ira . . ."?

Make your reader an authority frequently, and you will have a vigorous, well-read paper. Readers want information that they can share with others. That information makes them important. They can broadcast your news. You may be able to predict which information they need to make them broadcasters if you stand back and look at the subject from the reader's point of view. If you were a reader, what information would you want to tell someone else?

3. What surprised me when I was reporting the story?

Anything that surprised you will usually surprise, interest, and inform the reader. It often helps to take a few moments to reconstruct what you thought the story would be before you went out and did your reporting and then to compare that with what you learned. What you learned is often what the reader needs to learn in the lead.

4. Can you find an anecdote that captures the essence of the story?

Once I had a magazine editor tell me to write the way the Bible is written, in parables. I laughed at the time. Yes, he was an ordained minister; yes, he was a *Reader's Digest* editor. But it's not bad advice. Readers often see a story most clearly in brief anecdotes that include all the elements of narrative: character, place, dialogue, action, and reaction. Anecdotes capture and persuade the reader because they show instead of tell. They get the writer out of the way and put the reader on the scene.

Remember, however, that an anecdote lead is so powerful it may force the direction of the story. A marvelous anecdote that is just a bit off the line that should lead to the heart of the story will drag the whole piece off course. The anecdote in the lead must clarify the main issue in the story.

5. Have you an image that reveals the meaning of the story?

Often one detail that the writer can make the reader see will capture the meaning. We can show the reader the shoe on the highway after the ambulance has driven away, the tails of the rats the children have killed in the tenement, the nonhandshake of the political candidates just off the debate stage. A revealing image may not only give the writer a good lead but it may be something that can be woven through the whole story, repeated once or twice or three times, so that it helps hold a complicated story together.

6. Where is the conflict?

Good stories are often dramatic, and they can be told best by illustrating the actions and reactions of conflicting people or forces. It may help to play movie director and look for the center of dramatic conflict, so that you can reveal it to the reader in the lead.

Sometimes we can discover that center of conflict by diagramming the forces at work on scrap paper. If we draw circles around the territories of the participants in the story we may see where they intersect. Sometimes arrows showing where the forces are headed will lead to the intersection where the story should begin.

7. How will this news affect my readers?

Too often we write a story without letting our readers know how the story affects them, particularly in running political stories or technical stories written by specialists. We get so close to those stories and work so hard to make their complexities clear that we forget to tell our readers what the story means to them.

8. What's going on?

It may help to stand back for a moment to see the flow of events that is producing this story. Occasionally a lead can place the reader in the flow to be carried along on the campaign trail, in the investigation, out of the dressing room, onto the field. Such a lead allows the reader to understand the story by appreciating it.

9. Why should anyone read the story?

This is an essential question to ask yourself, especially at the *Globe* where projects go on long enough to have a life of their own. The reader may be forgotten during weeks of extensive reporting, writing, editing, and rewriting. Ask yourself why the reader should read the story, and you may recover the purpose and direction that the story has lost and find a pertinent lead as well.

10. Is there a metaphor to capture the story?

Our language gets much of its vigor from metaphors, and the right metaphor may focus a diffuse story. But metaphors are dangerous. A metaphor that is clever but not true forms a dishonest lead and a dishonest story. When I was on *Time* I sometimes felt that the senior editors (senior rewriters) would choose the metaphor over the story. It was not a good way to go.

11. Where does the story take place?

Readers in a television age especially like to see where the story takes place. A writer can top the stock television shots that usually fill our screen.

In writing a descriptive scene be aware of the dominant impression you wish to convey. Descriptions are not written effectively if they move from left to right or top to bottom. The details should lead someplace. You can make the reader see the pol, the cigar, the face, the belly, the left hand on one person's shoulder, the right hand grabbing another person's hand, the eyes focused on a third person. Everything in that description should reveal the dominant impression of the politician as a superficial gladhander.

Effective description will include, when it is appropriate, all the senses. The reader, through the writer, should not only be able to see the story, but also hear it, feel it, smell it, and taste it.

12. What is the appropriate voice for this story?

Voice, the way the story sounds, is the distinctive element in the story that gives the illusion of individual writer speaking to individual reader. It is the element of the story that carries its emotional force. The story may be detached, angry, humorous, caring, sarcastic, ironic, sad, amused. The whole range of human emotions is available to the writer using voice.

Journalism once attempted to achieve a single voice as if an institution were speaking. Today journalism not only allows increasingly diverse voices, it encourages them so that the reader hears writers speaking. It is our responsibility as writers to develop a range of voices with which we feel comfortable, and then to try them out by drafting leads to see which one will work best on a story. If we discover the voice then we usually have the lead.

13. Can we put a face on the story?

We all know that readers like to read about people, yet we appear to forget this truism in writing a lead. If we can get a person at center stage in the first paragraph we can get the reader's attention to a complicated and otherwise unreadable story.

Putting a face on the story, however, doesn't mean just name, age, address, occupation. We have to reveal that person in action in a place, so that the reader can see and believe the person.

14. Where is the tension in the story?

Many stories are best told by depicting tension between forces. This approach is significantly different from conflict, in which forces attack each other. Dramatic tension is created when two forces try to pull apart and yet can't free themselves from each other—a description that fits many marriages. If we can discover that such tension is vital to our story then we may find a lead that has insight and drama.

15. Is there a quote that tells the story?

The effective quotation lead allows the writer to get out of the way and let someone in the story reveal the primary issue in that person's own language. The quote that is attributed to someone else can make a statement that the objective reporter can not make. And the quote lead allows the reader to hear another voice.

The danger, of course, is that the writer will use a dramatic quotation that is not vital to the story; the quote sends the reader off on a false scent. The quote lead is such a powerful device that the writer must be sure it is honest and on target.

16. Which elements in the story connect? And how?

It is a principal responsibility of the artist and the journalist to make connections. The best leads often come to us when we explore the significant relationships within the story. To see these relationships in a complicated story it often helps to list the people, institutions, ideas, issues, and facts in a story, and then draw arrows and lines connecting them until you see a significant pattern of relationships.

17. What is the shape of the story?

Many writers, of whom John Updike is one, find the design of a story by visualizing it. One nonfiction book I wrote had me stuck for weeks until I saw the book as a series of concentric circles. I visualized these circles moving away from a center, as they would if you tossed a stone into a still pond. Once I saw that, I tossed the stone—my lead—and the book was started. A novel of mine didn't work until I saw it as a series of interacting fever charts and, therefore, understood how the paths of the characters crossed. I have written articles that are stairsteps, cones growing out from a point or drawing everything into a point, ladders, or a stack of boxes. Once you see the design you may be able to recognize the point where the reader can enter it, and you have the lead.

18. What generalization can be made about the story?

John Steinbeck used a three-by-five-inch card to set down what his novel was about. Sometimes when I've hunted for a lead I find it helpful to do the same thing, to write a simple précis, a sentence or two stating what the story will say. Occasionally, particularly if I'm writing an interpretive or analytic piece, that sentence or two becomes the lead. But more often it is a generalization that helps me focus the story, and when I have the focus I have the lead.

19. What key questions must be answered in the story?

Usually fewer than five questions have to be answered in the story. We can predict which question the reader will ask first, and the answer to that question may become the lead.

Most of the time we don't give the reader the question—the question is in the reader's mind—we just deliver the answer. Occasionally, however, the question or questions can be the lead. Dick Stewart used this technique in the *Globe* on August 21, 1980 in starting a very complicated legal story.

How was Levy Hart shot?

And how did he suffer a massive skull fracture?

These two central questions into the death of the 14-year-old Roxbury youth remain unanswered in the four volumes of inquest transcript released yesterday.

20. What is the best form for this story?

Form can be a lens through which we see a story. Sometimes it helps to change lenses and look at the subject in a different way. What if this hard news story were written as narrative? What if this normally soft lead story had a hard news lead? What if the story were told in the first person? When we have found the proper lens—the form—we may discover the lead.

21. How can I summarize this story?

Some stories need to fit under an umbrella, a sentence or two of summary that includes all the diverse aspects of the story. The umbrella lead is often an introduction to a quick bulleted list of the key ideas in the story.

22. Do you have a specific or two that reveals the significance of the story?

To find a good lead we should search our notes for the concrete detail, the fact, or the statistic that contains the essence of the story. If we find such a detail then we should give it to the reader in the lead. It will catch the reader's attention, and we can use the story to document its significance.

23. What is the story's history?

Journalists are all historians—without the advantage of hindsight. Good leads often come when we put an event into its proper historical framework, something print journalism can do that electronic journalism rarely attempts. The historical approach often works well when our readers know from radio or television what has happened but don't know where the event fits into a historical context. That point may be a good lead.

24. What point of view should the story be told from?

Point of view does not mean opinion. Think of the writer standing beside the reader and pointing out the story. The point of view is the place from which the reader can most effectively see the story. It may be on the street corner, in the police car, before the judicial bench, in the cell, beside the victim at the hospital, at the funeral home, in the parents' kitchen. Each story can be seen from many points of view, and when we are lead-hunting we should circle the story in our mind's eye, clicking off quick pictures until we find the one that helps our reader see the importance of the story. And that's our lead.

25. What are the problems to be solved in writing the story?

Studies of the creative process have shown that the creative person is identified not so much by the ability to see solutions as the ability to see problems. It often helps to look for the problems that have to be solved by writing the story. These technical problems may be how to show the lasting price of rape without exposing the victim to a kind of journalistic rape; how to make a complex fiscal report's effect on the reader clear; how to reveal the lobbyist's part in getting a bill passed. If we define the problem clearly we may discover the lead. Sometimes the definition of the problem is itself the lead.

26. What is the central event in the story?

In covering a series of events that take place during a story we may forget that one event—the speech at the Attleboro Rotary, the reverse on the 9-yard line—may be more important than any other. When we can find the key event we may have found the lead.

27. What is my opinion of the story?

It often helps to have your own opinion about what you are covering, even if it is not an opinion story. This does not mean a lack of objectivity in writing the story; just the opposite. We must know our own prejudices to be able to write fairly. The way we feel about the story, however, may reveal the story's significance to us and, therefore, reveal the lead.

28. Should I tell the story?

Rarely should you use the first person in a news story, for the danger is that you will get between the story and the reader, and the reader will learn more about the writer than about the subject. But there are still times when using the "I" will give the story special authority and put the reader on the scene.

29. Why did this story happen?

Who, what, where, when, why? It is the why that increasingly matters in newspapers. The why is what we give the readers that radio or television fails to give. In more and more stories the *why* provides the lead.

30. What is the process?

Most best-selling novels give the readers an enormous serving of process. They tell the readers how social climbers climb, how spies spy, how Hollywood works backstage, how airports, hotels, or factories function. If we look at the essential process that took place in the story we will often find a lead that will attract and hold readers.

The Lead Writer's Checklist

After you have written your final lead and finished the draft of the entire story, read the lead again to make sure it is:

Quick. The reader will decide to read on, or not to read on, in a matter of seconds.

Specific. Concrete details, precise quotes, or revealing facts.

Accurate. The reader who spots even a tiny error will refuse to believe anything you write.

Appropriate. Does this lead fit the story you have written, not the one you hoped to write?

Simple. Cut back the underbrush. Use proper nouns, active verbs, and concrete details.

Heard. Does the reader hear an individual writer speaking directly to the reader?

Honest. Can you deliver what you promise?

TWELVE

WRITING LIVELY

Lively writing should be built on accurate, perceptive reporting. We attract and hold readers when we collect and deliver reliable information they need in a manner that reveals its importance to them.

A few editors place liveliness ahead of significance. That shouldn't happen; nothing is as lively as a true, revealing fact. Lively writing doesn't have to be superficial, glib, or constructed with tricks to fool the reader. Glitter gets dull quickly—spend seventy-two hours in Las Vegas. Liveliness that wears well is simple, clear, and appropriate to the subject. It follows George Orwell's counsel, "Good writing is like a windowpane."

Lively Writing Improves Reporting

City room traditionalists, who often haul as much theology to work as members of the Curia, talk as if lively writing was a sin. They place reporting far over on the right and writing equally far to the left. If the two meet, they are in conflict—"Just give me the facts, Ma'am."

Lively writing, like all effective writing, depends directly on skillful and plentiful reporting. You can't write nothing, although many of us have tried. The writer depends on the careful selection of information from an abundant inventory collected by the reporter.

The reporter/writer shouldn't be schizophrenic. There shouldn't be reporting and then writing. The two activities should be integrated, with the reporter writing in the mind and on the screen while reporting and continuing to report while writing. The emphasis moves from one to the other, but they are not separate tasks.

Each city room has reporters who are not effective writers, but the really effective writers over the years are always good reporters. Their writing depends on specific, interesting, accurate information, and, in fact, their awareness of what the text will need gives focus to their reporting. They ask the reader's questions before the draft is written.

Writing Lively: Vision

Lively writing begins with the way in which the reporter/writer sees the world. Writing depends on our making the effort—often just a small effort—to see the story we are covering in a different light. But not for difference's sake. We move to a different angle of vision to see the story more clearly, more accurately, and to understand better what we see so that we can make our reader understand.

Wonder at the Commonplace

It is not our job to wander around wide-eyed and gap-mouthed as if we had just come down from New Hampshire and seen the tall buildings for the first time; it is our job to see the significant in what appears insignificant or commonplace to others. The novel I'm working on really began when I saw myself writing, "I had an ordinary war." When I read that back to myself I was astonished as I remembered what becomes ordinary in combat, and the novel began to force itself upon me.

We need to cultivate and maintain a certain innocence about the world and try to protect ourselves from the cynicism and know-it-allness that so often blinds the journalist. We have to be open to experience, to record and call attention to what our readers are passing by every day. When we do that they are surprised and delighted. We help them to see their world with new eyes.

Circle the Subject

It is our responsibility to circle the story; not just to wrap it in a journalistic cliché, but to move around to see what's really happening. It may be a straight news story of a mugging, but that straight news story may be best told from the point of view of the victim, the mugger, the police, the victim's family, the mugger's family, the passive or active observer, the social worker, the sociology professor, the district or defense attorney, and so on.

We may understand the story better if we put ourselves, for a moment, in the mind of each of the people involved. We might play with time, for example, and find a way to report on how muggers plan, how they arm themselves, and how they identify a victim; or we might leap ahead and see what they do with the loot or how a mugging changes the life of a victim.

We are on a continual search for the way we can best serve our readers. Where is the story that will reveal the information that they need to know?

Use a Zoom Lens

One writer always tells the human story, focusing on one mugging, one victim. Another writer steps back and reports each mugging the same way, always telling it as a traditional news story, with detachment, complete with a hard news lead or a delayed lead followed quickly by a nut graph. A third writer always goes for the big picture, reporting on violence in western civilization, past, present, and future. We all get into habits of vision. We take close-ups, or stay in a middle distance, or always go for the long shot.

A good way to get out of such a bad habit (which can be an institutional habit of the paper or a department on the paper) is to imagine a zoom lens and to move in quickly, then back, to see where this particular story lies. There is no right way to tell a story in the abstract. Each story demands its own telling.

Where's the Fight?

Lively writing often results from finding the point at which the people or the issues in the story are in conflict. The problem is that we all too quickly learn the stereotype for the court story, the press conference, the profile, the game story, the feature, the editorial, or the column. We look for the information that fits the stereotype and forget to search for the moment of tension at which the particular energy of this story is released.

If we search for the true point of conflict we will serve our readers better, and we will have readers, for they will want to see what happens.

There is nothing like a good fight to attract our attention. We shouldn't start fights or make them up, but if we see forces, or people, heading for each other we should get into position to cover the collision.

What's the Context?

It's quite possible to produce a dull story filled with potentially interesting information. We don't put the story into context; we don't let the reader see what the story means or how it will affect the reader.

Many stories float right off the page. There's nothing wrong with them; in fact, some of them can be almost technically perfect, but they do not connect with the world of the reader. It is our task not just to report information, but to put it into a context that reveals its significance.

Make Them Walk

Yes, readers want to read about people, and so many newspapers, our own included, fill stories with names that pop up like targets on an FBI shooting range. Readers need names and ages and professions and addresses, but they need much more than that. Readers want to meet people on the page who can be seen.

We should try to reveal the characters in a story in action and remember when we do that the action should relate to the story and advance the reader's understanding.

Hear Them Talk

Newspapers are filled with quotetalk. It has quotation marks around it and is connected to the text with a "he said" or "she said," but it is a language no one has ever heard. And it is the same for all characters in all stories, despite their differences in age, education, social background, racial heritage, or regional location.

We must listen to those we quote and then capture their speech so that our pages are filled with the music of different voices, a music that is lively but, more than that, reveals what is being said and how it is being said.

Writing Lively: Information

We will have readers if we give people the information that will make them authorities. When a reader gets a specific piece of information—

exactly how much larger Dolly Parton's head has become as the rest of her has gotten smaller—the reader delights in passing that information along. The reader becomes, in a Scottish term for gossip, a broadcaster.

Writing is lively for our readers if they can be the person at the office or the supermarket or the kitchen table who can reveal an interesting detail about a public person, a vote or an election, a strike, a game or trade, a stock market move, a trend, a scandal, a new vacation spot. Our readers are hungry for information, and we will attract new readers if we earn a reputation for delivering tasty facts.

Accuracy of Fact

But they must be accurate. If we deliver the wrong information to the reader, and the reader uses it to establish his or her authority and then finds the fact is wrong, the reader is humiliated, and eventually we lose the reader.

The scholar's authority comes from footnotes, and in many cases our authority comes from attribution. But we should remember that is not always true. In many stories our authority comes from the reader when we articulate a feeling or concern the reader has, and that reader says, "Yes, that's right."

Accuracy of Context

We should never forget what I said above: Accuracy is not only a matter of fact, but of context.

Revealing Details

Too often writers, in an effort to lighten up, will spray their stories with specifics. Every profile subject puffs on a cigarette; every action is described in a specific, statistical manner; each face has a quote. I try to test the specifics from which I build my story by looking for revealing details, the concrete material that, piece by piece, reveals the story. The key word is *reveals*. Each detail should show the reader a bit more of the story.

The pressure to process information and publish it in the paper is enormous. One way we accomplish this task is to pour the information, like concrete, into preconstructed forms. We are often assigned to write a form such as a profile, a wrap-up, a hard news story, or a feature. The system works. In fact, it works too well. We often see what is going on in terms of the story it will fit. All writers can cite cases in which they have a struggle to make a story fit an editor's preconception. They are not aware, however, how many times they see only what they need to see to produce a certain type of story.

On deadline it may be necessary to fit the story to a familiar form. But the paper that is written and edited in a lively way will encourage writers when they have the time to allow the form of the story to arise from its facts.

Form is Meaning

We should not overlook the fact that form is meaning. The form itself communicates a message. The inverted pyramid says that there is immediate information the reader needs to know; the profile speaks to the importance of a single person in making the news; and the event story presupposes a significant event.

If we look at the world with honest eyes, we may see stories that have been invisible to us before, and by writing them in a form that is appropriate to the information we have to communicate, we will share an important meaning with our readers.

The reader, of course, does not put a name on the form of the story being read. But the reader will sense a discomfort if the form of the story does not fit the facts. And the reader, on the other hand, will believe and delight in a story in which the form illuminates a significant meaning.

Short or Long?

As short as possible, that is the rule. Too often reporters and their story editors equate status with the number of trees destroyed in Canada. Readers want stories that are short but filled with an adequate serving of information. The length of the story should come from the amount of information the reader needs and the space it takes to put that information into an accurate and appropriate context.

Getting From Here to There

Lively writing usually allows the reader to participate in the story. The reader has a sense of discovery. At each point in the story the reader has a question answered, but a new question grows out of that: Will they meet? Will they see each other again? Will they move in together? Will they marry? Will they have children? Each story has its own sequence.

We should use the natural organization of the story. We may, for example, tell the story as a story, using narrative to pull the reader through a series of confrontations. A story may be organized by time, by geography, by cause and effect, or by problem and solution. We should look for the sequence that serves the reader best.

If the story is complicated or the form different from what the reader expects, then we may serve the reader by telling the reader what we are doing and why ("This is the story of a complex series of bureaucratic decisions in which good people are doing good and causing harm"). Sometimes this can be done by using the reader's questions as crossheads and then answering them. Other times we can have the clock ticking right in the story or use any other device that helps the reader through the information so that they will understand the significant relationships that build to a final meaning.

Writing Lively: Voice

Lively writing ultimately depends on voice. When we think about voice we usually think of an individual writer's voice, because those writers who are most successful have developed a distinctive voice, a way of speaking that is natural for them, hopefully appropriate to the subject they are writing about, and interesting to a reader.

This emphasis on the individual voice or style can be dangerous. The writer can be a prisoner of a distinctive voice, and a beginning writer can reach for a voice that isn't natural or appropriate. And yet, the quality of voice is central to lively writing. Readers hear the stories they read; they like the heard quality of writing, the sense of a personal conversation with the writer.

The Voice of the Text

I have come to believe that the best way to think about voice is not to emphasize the personal voice of the writer or the institutional voice of the publication, but to focus on the voice of the story. If we think of the voice that is appropriate to the story, then we can blend the personal or natural voice of the writer and the institutional or professional voice of the paper to produce a voice that reinforces the meaning of the story.

Talking With the Reader

Not at the reader, not to the reader, but with the reader, conversationally, using the pace and emphasis and music that is appropriate to the bad or good or complex or hilarious information we are sharing. To make writing more lively it may be helpful to turn off the screen so that you are forced to hear what you are writing. The ear is our most effective editor. But more than that, if we are to have writing that is heard by our readers, we need to put that aural element into the writing.

Voice as Meaning

We should remember that what was true of form, that the shape of the piece communicates a meaning, is just as true of voice. The voice of a text is what causes (most of the time) the reader to believe the text to understand the importance of what is being said. Writing is music, after all; not music to decorate, but music to communicate, to reveal meaning.

We should also remember that the voice of the draft often reveals the meaning of the story or its importance to the writer. I listen carefully to what I am saying and how I am saying it. If I sound detached, for example, when I should be involved, or involved when I should be detached, I believe that the text is trying to tell me something. As I write, my concern, my anger, my unhappiness, and my sense of humor are all unleashed by my voice. I must harness and use them to serve the reader.

Voice, form, information, and vision are all used to produce lively writing. We should, however, remember what Hemingway told us, "Prose is architecture, not interior decoration." Our business is not entertainment, although it's no crime to be entertaining; our business is to reveal the world to the reader. Lively writing will produce the specific information, the appropriate forms, the interesting voices that will reveal what is wrong, what is right, what has happened, what will happen, what needs to be changed, and why and how. We write lively to get attention and to deserve that attention by what we deliver to the reader.

THIRTEEN

LET'S GET ORGANIZED

What do you do when you've got 172 notes, twenty-seven interviews, 223 clips, fourteen pamphlets, twenty-two speeches, eight charts, 338 press releases, thirteen reports, eight memos from the editor, and a draft that rides off in nine directions at once? Here are four techniques that may help:

1. Say one thing

The greatest problem in news writing is the story that lacks focus. The writer tries to say two, three, or thirty-seven things of equal importance. An effective news story has one dominant meaning. The writer, the editor, and the reader have to know that meaning.

To discover the meaning you have to get disentangled from all your notes and clips. I like to take a note pad and sit in a comfortable chair where I can't even see the notes and try to write down the one thing the story must say. I try to do it in a sentence, but sometimes it doesn't need to be a sentence. It can simply be a phrase: "more taxes," "rape victim raped by publicity." Once I have that sentence or phrase I have a North Star to guide me.

I still do not return to my notes. I list the most important points that document or develop the main point of the article. When I have that point I put them in order and draft the piece from this outline, not going back to my notes until I have a draft done. You have to stand back from the clutter and see the points that are significant to a reader.

Saul Pett, one of the Associated Press's best writers, may spend days putting his notes in piles to accomplish the same purpose. I think most expert writers of long pieces find the time spent stacking and restacking notes, clips, releases, and so on valuable in solving organizational problems before they create a draft that looks like a train wreck.

If the train wreck has occurred, it may be helpful to get a printout and cut it apart paragraph by paragraph. Then play solitaire with the paragraphs, rearranging the mosaic until it supports the main point.

But you can't do anything until you've found the North Star, the one dominant point you want to make in the draft.

2. Draft many leads—or ends

Another way to find the focus of a piece of writing is to write as many leads or ends as you can as quickly as possible: twenty, thirty, forty, sixty leads. Sixty is about normal for me on an article. I may use the third one, but after sixty I know the third one is good.

These leads or ends shouldn't be written carefully. They should take about three minutes each. They play off each other. Many are silly, and most won't work. But each will trigger other leads or ends, other ways to get hold of the subject.

Each lead explores a direction, a focus, a voice that may work. Each lead—or end—is a draft or sketch of the entire piece, in a sense. The experienced writer can see in those few lines the whole.

Drafting leads or even endings can be a deadline technique. The time invested to draft just a half a dozen leads pays good returns if you find the right lead instead of stumbling through a piece following the false directions of a bad lead.

3. Ask the reader's questions

Every good story is a conversation with an individual reader. The reader asks questions that do not appear in the text. Your text is an answer to those questions.

Again, if you have a complicated story, get away from the notes and list the five or so questions the reader will ask. They should not be the questions you hope the reader will ask, but the ones, like it or not, the reader will ask. Once you have those questions you can anticipate the order in which they will be asked: How much will the MTA fare increase be? When? Why? How else can I travel to work? Any way I can start a repeal movement?

If you have to rewrite or edit a draft that is incoherent or confused, you can use the same technique to stand back and look at what is important to the reader.

If you have problems standing back—getting outside your own perspective—it may help to role-play a reader. Imagine yourself a specific person, someone who is intelligent but a bit dense and who certainly does not know the subject. Your brother-in-law Arnold, for example. Let Arnold ask the questions. Those are the questions you're going to have to answer. A lot of Arnolds are out there.

4. Seek a natural order

Today many stories do not fit the inverted pyramid in which the order is of decreasing importance to the reader. That order, first news first, second news second, third news third, can still work, but many other choices are available to the writer.

The natural order is the one in which the story can best be told. The reader is carried along easily from point to point. There is no need for transitions, a device meant to make it possible to wrench information out of the natural order and present it to the reader. Transitions are always clumsy; try to find an order that makes them unnecessary.

Here are some forms of natural order that can be used in newspapers today.

- **Chronology**. Time is the thread that holds the story together. Events are recreated following the order in which they occurred, and the reader is allowed to have the feeling of time passing—years, months, weeks, days, hours, seconds—whatever is appropriate to the story.

Michael Kenney used chronology skillfully in this lead:

The Monday morning after Christmas vacation, Lorene Younis's teachers noticed raw, open sores on the 13-year-old girl's body, apparently only the most recent occasion when they suspected the North Attleboro girl was being abused by her parents.

As they had on several occasions, school officials notified the Public Welfare Department. This time, according to sources, they insisted that a social worker come to the junior high school and see the girl's condition for herself.

Yesterday, the girl's father, George J. Younis, a 37-year-old offset print-

er, was arraigned in Attleboro Superior Court on 15 counts of assault and battery, 12 counts of mayhem, 15 counts of kidnapping, one count of non-support and 12 counts of being an accessory to assault and battery.

Notice that Kenney gets to the hard news by the third paragraph. A delayed lead means a short delay. Readers should certainly know the context of the story by the third paragraph.

- **The trip.** Many stories can be organized by taking the reader along on a trip with the news source. This may be a campaign spin, a walk through a prison, a visit to a neighborhood, anywhere with a natural movement across territory. The reader is carried along by this movement, and the information readers need is hung along the clothesline of action.

Maria Karagianis used this technique to help the reader see the problems of maintaining Boston State Hospital.

At Boston State Tuesday, it had just started to snow. Driving across the grounds, past empty brick dormitories and a boarded-up morgue, past a cricket field choked with weeds and an abandoned laundry, Jerry O'Connor was talking about the difficulties of administering such a place.

He was talking about the packs of wild dogs that roam about, the rats and roaches, the high crime rate in the neighborhood and the constant muggings and car thefts.

"These institutions are beyond their time," he said. "The place to serve citizens best is in their own communities, in their neighborhoods, not in those huge, old dilapidated buildings."

- **The search.** We are carried along on the search for a suspect, a new product, a vote. The exposition is inserted where we need it to understand the search.
- **Problem and solution.** The reader shares the problem of the scientist, the engineer, the field commander, and the coach and then takes part in the attempt to find a solution.
- **Narrative.** The writer uses the ancient skills of telling a story to allow a series of meaningful events to unfold. The story moves forward along with the action and reaction of the participants.

FOURTEEN

ANALYSIS OF A MICHAEL KRANISH STORY

To learn how to organize my stories, I pasted up a printed version of the story on the left-hand side of the page and wrote down by each paragraph how it contributed, or did not contribute, to the growth of the story.

I also did the same thing to stories I admired, trying to find out why and how they worked. This is what I have done to a fine story by Michael Kranish of the *Globe*'s Washington Bureau.

ALEXANDRIA, Va.—On a desolate dead-end street, sandwiched between the National Linen Service and the Wild and Wooly Needlepoint store, the Nixon Presidential Materials Project is buried in a nondescript warehouse, an ignoble monument to the president who resigned in disgrace 15 years ago today.

A fine lead that is built from revealing specifics and puts the story in context. It is a long sentence for a newspaper, but it flows clearly and gracefully. I hear the writer speaking. Kranish promises me more interesting information if I read on. I did.

"So," said an archivist pleasantly, "do you want to listen to the 'smoking gun' tape?"

Notice how quickly Kranish sets a tone of casualness, unexpected by the reader for such a place. And how quickly we move to the central issue. Kranish has anticipated the reader's question, "Will I be able to hear THE tape?" and answered it immediately.

This is the only place in the world where the Watergate tapes can be heard, where The Voice, that raspy Nixon voice, conspires and curses until his presidency collapses. *"I want you to stonewall it, let them plead the Fifth Amendment, cover up or anything else . . ."*

Kranish moves back and puts the place in context and then makes you HEAR the voice on the tape. He delivers the quote. That line, "conspires and curses until his presidency collapses," is one I wish I had written. It is active and covers a whole period in history in a few well-chosen words.

In this era of the Nixon comeback, of grand presidential libraries in spectacular settings, this is history's revenge. Congress did not trust the Nixon presidential materials to anyone but the National Archives, so the Nixon Annex on Pickett Street, costing $800,000 per year, was born. Congress decided that Nixon's own library, under construction in California, will have none of the tapes, papers or momentoes, which means that the Nixon there will be far different from the Nixon here.

I am impressed by how much information he packs into three clear, running sentences. He gives us specific information ($800,000), delights us with a meaningful phrase ("history's revenge"), and makes the significance of what he has told us clear at the end of the paragraph, the point of greatest emphasis.

This is the sole government storehouse of 40 million pages of Nixon presidential material, such a massive collection that the 23 bureaucrats here have only sorted through about

Specifics and news combined. Each word counts.

10 percent of it. Nixon, perhaps, still obsessed with secrecy, has kept much of the material from public view and is seeking to keep more of it private.

Yesterday, a few visitors sat in the archives' Listening Room, dominated by a large, black-and-white portrait of a smiling Nixon, and listened.

Now he sets the scene.

Marie Pierce, 21, a British tourist who read about the archives in a travel guide called *Let's Go: USA,* pulled on a pair of headphones and heard John Dean tell Nixon, *"We have a cancer within, close to the presidency, that is growing."*

Wonderful. We hear the tapes through the ears of someone from another country who is too young to have listened to the hearings. And we are given a sample quote.

"This cancer-on-the-presidency is the best tape so far," Pierce said, marveling at a conversation that changed the course of American history.

I learn from the way he adjusts the distance of his text, moving in close to give the story immediacy, moving back to put it in context. Too often we keep the camera at the same distance all the time.

Indeed, the political surreal is the rule here at "The Nixon Project," as it is called. In room after room, thousands of files labeled "John Dean" and "John Ehrlichman" are stored in special acid-free boxes. The archivists are ever alert to the possibility of, pardon the expression, a break-in. Security guards man the building 24 hours a day; the alarm is so sensitive it has been set off by a fly. No one wants a third-rate burglary.

And there is much to tempt the uninvited. If the storage of the tapes and papers is little known, then it is a vital secret that the 30,000 gifts to Nixon during his presidency are also stored in a back room that is not open to the public. There is the exquisite box with a portrait of Nixon and his wife, Pat, that was given to the president by a Soviet leader; the magnificent diamond and emeralds given by a Saudi prince; and the plastic, glow-in-the-dark set of hands clasped in prayer. From the extravagant to the odd, it is all here under the supervision of curator Wally Owen, who puts on white gloves before he touches any of the treasured items.

Notice how he orders his list from the expected to the surprisingly tacky. And the gloves are a nice touch. There is almost always a nice tension in each paragraph, such as the tackiness of the treasures and the respect with which they are treated.

"It is really a shame that there is no museum for this," Owen said, as he caressed a baseball glove that was signed, "Richard Nixon."

Kranish could have been heavy handed here, but he gets out of the way and lets Owen self-destruct. Nice verb "caressed."

But in truth, few people come here for the tapes, the transcripts or the treasures. The majority want Elvis. The Nixon Presidential Material Project so far has sold 12,000 copies of photos showing Presley, wearing a giant belt buckle and shirt open halfway to his navel, shaking hands with Nixon. No other item comes close in popularity.

Surprise is at the center of lively writing. Not tricky, hokey, made-up surprise but reported and revealed surprise put in a context that gives it meaning. Kranish doesn't write this paragraph. He follows Orwell's counsel and does not call attention to himself but becomes a "windowpane" and lets us see the story.

The archives forget nothing. At that meeting Presley gave Nixon a .45 caliber pistol, now duly stored and catalogued. Indeed, the biggest news to come out of the Nixon papers recently was that Presley asked to become a federal agent-at-large for the Bureau of Narcotics and Dangerous Drugs. The appointment was never made.

Again, another surprise and an effective understatement at the end. Get off stage. The job is done.

Try this yourself. Pick the best story you've written recently and figure out, paragraph by paragraph, how you did it.

FIFTEEN

Interview:
SALLY JACOBS

I keep clipping Sally Jacobs' stories. Her work is marked for me by a mastery of the professional skills we should all have with an ability to push the limits of those skills, so that her stories have a special impact that doesn't draw attention to her, but to the story.

How do you get a reader to read?

Every time I start a story I think of that picture of the middle-aged couple sitting at the breakfast table. The man, reading the paper, suddenly drops his coffee cup, nearly collapses into his wheat germ, and explains to his wife, "Good God, Martha! Did you read this?"

I would, of course, like everybody to react to my stories that way and then refuse to budge until they have read to the bitter end. In the real world, to get them involved in the first few paragraphs, I try to create as powerful and vivid a picture as I can, something that promises of what to come without promising more than it can deliver.

A "soft lead" is wrong for many spot stories, but the alternative is not always the five W's capped by a "he said." I try hard to avoid that kind of lead; instead, I come up with a line or two that tells readers just as much as a conventional lead but with more electricity.

There's really no way to describe how to do that, but if there is I wish someone would tell me. Generally, I find that what strikes me personally as funny or curious works well as a lead.

What do you try to do, and not do, when drafting a story?

I keep thinking about George and Martha. I figure I've got to make up for the coffee he spilled and try hard to keep the action going in the story.

With a really great tale, the story stays alive on its own. More often, you've got to work, to alternate form, to gradually unleash your information and color, to keep it going. Although you've told the reader pretty much what to expect up high in the story, you've got to hold back in order to keep the tension alive.

How to do that well, of course, is the trick.

How do you get ideas for stories?

I find the problem is not so much getting ideas for stories as it is choosing from among the many stories I'd like to do. Some of the best stories, of course, are not the great exposé of wrongdoing or badness but the simple event, the person or weird happening that often doesn't appear to be a story at first glance.

I try to talk regularly with people who are familiar with the areas I'm interested in, like criminal justice and social services, and usually those conversations generate at least a few ideas. Inmates and people on the receiving end of state services usually know of situations even stranger than their own.

What are the elements of a story idea that make it worthwhile for you to pursue it?

I have a keen interest in oddballs and weirdos, which, as any reporter knows, include just about everybody. This is an appetite that grows sharper with the years and means I know not what.

I like stories with distinct, colorful characters, which I think not only help to order a story, but make it more fun for readers. The fact that they have come to my or the *Globe*'s attention often means that they are at odds with society or one of its symptoms, which generally constitutes the tension in the story.

How do you get people to talk to you?

There are sprinkled among humanity some people who consider reporters a step on the evolutionary scale below roaches and wouldn't tell you if your back was on fire. But I find that most people want to talk and, in fact, am constantly amazed at the emotions and intimacies that people gab about to the media.

With people less inclined, I try to offer something of myself, to show a knowledge and understanding of their situation that may make them more willing. Most important, I try to be patient. Deadlines can make one impatient with a reluctant interview, but I find that usually people just need a little time and conversation before they are willing to talk.

What note-taking techniques are most valuable to you?

Writing legibly is a continual challenge. I confess, there have been times in the past when I have gone to write a story several weeks after an interview and have been convinced that I, or the person being interviewed, must have been on drugs. For years I have made myself go quickly over my notes soon after taking them in order to clarify in readable writing important quotes or comments.

I stress that I only do this with portions of the interview that I'm fairly confident I will use in the story, which is generally less than I expect. I find that the best way to capture a story on paper is to write quickly and largely from memory so as not to lose the pace, which does not allow for much time to leaf through a notebook. But I always try to skim my notes before and after writing to make sure I haven't missed something particularly colorful or revealing. Usually I have.

Tape recorders are even more problematic simply because they take too much time. By the time I've nailed down the phrase I thought I wanted, I've thought of a better way.

How can an editor best help you?

I came from a newspaper where editors could not rest easy at night unless they had rewritten a good part of your story and reporters made voodoo dolls of those able to sleep the soundest. Here, I find precisely the opposite problem.

To me, a good editor is not always the one who does the least, who waits for the story to show up and then keeps it at arm's length. I think editors need to be involved, to take time to talk to a reporter about an approach, about ideas, and the like, without dictating The Way. A lot of times I get my best ideas, or find out where I have holes in my thinking, in talking with an editor.

Too, when writing under pressure, any reporter may unintentionally make mistakes or take a shortcut. Although I write my stories the way I think they should run, I would far rather have someone tighten my copy if it needs it than have it run sloppy.

SIXTEEN

Interview:
BOB RYAN

The sports section of the Boston *Globe* has often been called the best in the country. As a sports nut who travels a great deal I find that true. The sports pages inform on a broad spectrum of sports. They combine feature and news, opinion and background, humor and technical information. These pages have shown that there is a place for the newspaper even when we have seen the event on television—even reseen and reseen and reseen it on instant replay—and then seen it on the late news and the early news. We still need good sports writers to tell us what we've seen. And one of the best of the best is Bob Ryan.

What techniques do you have for rehearsing or thinking about what you're going to write before you start writing?

I do a lot of structuring while driving. I think out line after line, and I've even been known to jot down a phrase or story line in my notebook, which is generally within reach on the front seat. I really get psyched up for major stories, and I work hard on my leads and endings beforehand. I seldom sit down to write anything important not having thought about it for days. Incidentally, I usually assume that any clever phrasing in the body of the story will come by itself. It's leads and endings I worry about.

Do you rewrite?

I'm starting to rethink my position on rewriting. I used to be doctrinaire and cocky: what I wrote I wrote, and that was it. I would edit, sure, but rewrite? Never. Obviously, I knew this was dangerous. Pure laziness accounted for much of it. I've written four books with a minimum of rewrite. Could I have improved them? Certainly.

How do you organize a complicated story?

God bless (a) parochial school and (b) prep school. Eight years of the former and five years of the latter gave me an irreplaceable background in the basics. I learned to outline in both places, and although I may not formally outline every major piece, I do outline most of them in at least a semistructured way. You've got to list major areas of your general subject matter; you simply cannot rely on memory. You need your lead, of course, and somewhere up high you've got to make a case for the story being written at all. What makes him/her/them/it special? Why now instead of last year? The reader deserves to know.

I never cease to be amazed that I can watch a game on television, fall asleep late, and find an account of the game in the Globe *delivered to my house in New Hampshire before 6:30 in the morning. I'd be interested in some of your tricks in writing to deadline.*

This is what I do best, he said, with no hint of modesty. The most important thing isn't a trick. If you don't know the game you can't write a great sports game story. I could finesse my way to a smooth hockey game story, but the aficionado of that sport will know I faked it, just the way basketball junkies know that, polysyllabic impressions aside, John Powers wasn't a real basketball man.

The most important aspect of writing game stories is access to information. A writer must have a comprehensible system of scorekeeping. Next, a writer must have a decent note-taking system, preferably one involving a spiral notebook that fits into an inside breast pocket (this may be the best reason to dress properly). The aim is to start writing with quick access to as much information as possible.

I start thinking about leads as soon as the game starts. Contingency leads can occasionally be formulated before the game starts, if a situation calls for it. I was sitting on a line for weeks prior to the seventh and final game of the 1974 Milwaukee–Boston NBA finals. I had occasionally envisioned it as the lead. Instead, I used it as the ending. It was, "How's the view from Olympus, boys?" There is a one-time-only line.

In an ideal situation, I have the basis of the lead ready by the time the game ends. Sometimes, however, it comes from post-game conversations in the locker room and sometimes from an overheard remark of another writer or a passerby. If nothing materializes prior to writing time, I sit and think awhile. If nothing clever comes then, I write a fairly standard wire-service type of lead and hope I can spice the story up with humor or profound technological insight.

It's nice if the ending ties in with the lead, but that doesn't happen all the time. About all that I ask of the ending is that it not be too contrived.

What I'm trying to do in a game story is to be informative, entertaining, and opinionated as hell. The old "five W's" are passé. I try to get the score in no later than the fourth paragraph. I editorialize, because if the *Globe* didn't want a point of view they'd rip the wire-service version from the wire. I want to impress both solid sports fans and just plain literate people. With the constrictions of a deadline it's a tremendous challenge to produce such a piece, and I am very proud of what I do.

What do you think of sportswriting compared to other newspaper writing?

The beauty of today's sportswriting is the freedom granted writers by newspapers, such as the *Globe*. The reason why the best overall writing done at the *Globe* is done in the sports pages (an opinion I would defend to the death) is that we get good space, aren't as worried about offending people, and aren't as knotted up with "propriety." Creativity is stifled elsewhere in the name of "taste." Yecch.

I'll tell you something else. Too much attention cannot be paid to the basics of grammar and rhetoric. I'm shocked at some things I see in our paper. Where are the desk men, I wonder? It scares me.

Draft:

Write for Surprise

W hen a first draft is going well I often feel I am racing downhill on a bicycle, the wheels moving so fast I have to take my feet off the pedals and stick them out, stiff legged, to keep my balance as I hurtle downhill, teetering, almost off balance, almost out of control—but not quite.

Velocity is essential to first-draft writing. It allows the writer to escape the critic for the moment; it causes surprise, the accidents of insight and language that are essential to effective writing.

The best writers do not come to the first draft, no matter how much they have rehearsed, with the draft thought out. Writing is thinking. The writer discovers what the writer has to say by writing. As E. M. Forster said, "How do I know what I think until I see what I say?"

A certain dumbness is an advantage in beginning the first draft. The draft will instruct; the act of writing organizes information into meaning, and that meaning is often a surprise. Even when the writer knows the story line (the election results, the final score, the suspect arrested) the writing of the story reveals a deeper meaning. Cause and effect, implication, historical context, process, problem, and solution come clear in the writing of a draft.

The writer often feels uncomfortable with surprise; the page is not producing what is expected by the editor or the writer. Sometimes that unexpected text needs to be rejected, but most of the time the real story lies within what has not been seen or thought of until it is exposed by the high-speed writing of the first draft, when the writer hurtles towards an unintended meaning.

SEVENTEEN

TRICKS OF THE WRITING TRADE

One day I made a list of what I wish I'd known before I showed up for my first job on a newspaper. Here it is:

1. Ask the Reader's Questions

Ask yourself the questions the reader will ask before you start reporting—not the questions you'd like them to ask, but the questions they will inevitably ask. Most stories can be told by answering five questions, give or take a question. Keep revising the questions as the story develops.

2. Collect Abundant Detail

Writing is a constant process of selection. The effective story can be told by the amount of good material you toss in the wastebasket. Use all your senses—sight, hearing, smell, taste, touch—to pack your notebook, and your memory, with specifics you may need when writing.

3. View Each Story From Different Points of View

Most journalists are predictable; they see every story the way every other journalist sees it. Joseph Conrad told us, "My task . . . is, by the written word, to make you hear, to make you feel . . . it is, above all, to make you see." Christopher Isherwood said, "I am a camera with its shutter open, quite passive, recording not thinking. Recording the man shaving at the window opposite and the woman in the kimono washing her hair. Some day, all this will have to be developed, carefully fixed, printed." Theodore Roethke commented, "Nothing seen, nothing said."

4. Enter the Skin of Your Sources

Yes, you will have to become detached (though not unconcerned) to write well, but you will not get the most important stories unless you develop the ability to empathize, to understand what the story is doing to the participants. This doesn't mean you approve or disapprove; it does mean that you understand.

5. Rehearse

While you are reporting, and after you finish reporting and head back to the office, write the story in your head. Play with words, phrases, and lines; listen to the music of the stories that may be written, because music nearly as often as facts can tell you what the story means.

6. Listen for the Initiating Line

Good writing usually begins with a line. It may be a sentence but often it is not. The line is a series of words that contain tension, or conflict, and music. The forces in the story are coiled within that line, just for a moment, eager to be released by the writing of the story. I will not write until I find that line, which may sound ordinary to others but has energy and resonance for me. Sometimes it is the lead, often it is not, but it ignites the draft.

7. Say One Thing

Effective stories have one dominant message. You may have to write a first draft to discover the message, but there should be a single meaning that has priority over all the other meanings in the story. If you can't tell the message in a sentence or less after you have written the final draft, you haven't written the final draft.

8. Write Many Leads to Find the Lead

Most reporters are hired on papers of the level of the *Globe* because they have written the best first leads wherever they have worked, but if they keep moving to better papers they will be surrounded by others who have written "best" leads. The breakthrough to top writer may come when the reporter writes many leads—ten, fifteen, twenty, or more—

taking three minutes or less for each draft lead during this essential play. The leads discarded will appear at key points in the story and at the end. Writing many leads may increase the speed with which a story is written as well as improve its quality.

9. Write Without Notes

Put your notes aside and write the first draft from memory. Follow the instinctive flow of the story so that you can make unexpected connections as well as expected ones. Check your notes afterwards for accuracy, but you will find that what you forget probably is best forgotten, and what you remembered in the flow of writing is what needs to be remembered.

10. Write Easily

Forced writing usually sounds like forced writing. Good writing should have the ease of good conversation. Find your way to tell the story without forcing it, letting it appear naturally. To do this you may have to write fast so that you can out race the censors who live within us all.

To produce writing worth criticism, remember William Stafford's counsel:

> I believe that the so-called "writing block" is a product of some kind of disproportion between your standards and your performance. . . . One should lower his standards until there is no felt threshold to go over in writing. It's easy to write. You just shouldn't have standards that inhibit you from writing.
>
> I can imagine a person beginning to feel he's not able to write up to that standard he imagines the world has set for him. But to me that's surrealistic. The only standard I can rationally have is the standard I'm meeting right now. . . . You should be more willing to forgive yourself. It doesn't make any difference if you are good or bad today. The assessment of the product is something that happens after you've done it.

11. Write With Your Ear

Writing that is read and remembered has the illusion of a speaking voice—an individual, human voice is heard. Put the heard quality into the writing by listening for the *voice of the text*. This is not the eccentric, self-indulgent voice of the writer or the traditional voice of the institution, but a mixture of many elements brought together in a voice that supports and illuminates the meaning of a story.

12. Write With Information

Writing that is full of meaning is not written with language, but information—specific, accurate, significant information. The reader wants to become an authority who can quote the concrete details, the statistics, the quotations you have delivered.

13. Reveal

"Show, don't tell" is the fiction writer's counsel. It's not bad advice for the journalist. Show and tell. Put the reader in the story and then, when the reader asks, "What's it mean?" tell the reader. It is our job to reveal the story to the reader, to make the reader experience the story, to cause the reader to think and feel. Get out of the way of the information and present it directly to the reader.

14. Vary the Documentation

Make the reader believe by giving the reader evidence at each point in the story. Most writers fall into the trap of using one form of documentation with which they have become comfortable. The documentation shouldn't fit the writer; rather, it should be appropriate to the point being made. Choose a quote, an anecdote, a statistic, a citation from a report, a description, or other evidence because it supports the point effectively.

15. Answer the Reader's Questions

You anticipated those questions before and during your reporting; now answer them. The most effective way to organize a story is to put those questions in the order the reader will ask them. A well-written, and well-read, story answers the reader's questions *when* they are asked.

16. Cut Anything That Doesn't Move the Story Forward

No interesting detail, no significant action, no great quote, no brilliant phrase belongs in the story if it doesn't advance the principal message of the story. All the stories within the story that give it depth and texture must relate to the main meaning of the story.

17. Stop in Mid-sentence When Interrupted

It is important to maintain the voice and flow of the story. The best way to do this is to stop when you know what is coming next, what you are saying, and how it may be said.

18. Be Accurate in Detail and Context

If one fact is wrong, the reader will not believe the whole story; however, accuracy is not just a matter of facts, but facts in context. Writing is a matter of selection, enormous selection, and we have the responsibility to make sure that our facts are accurate in relation to other facts and to the world of the story.

19. Be Your Own Editor

You know the world of the story better than any editor can. You have a professional obligation to your reader, your paper, and yourself to be your own editor. Stand back and role-play a specific reader—see and hear your story as that reader will.

It may be efficient to do three quick readings:

- Read for *meaning*. If you don't have one, there's no reason to go on. Find the meaning.

- Read for *structure*. If the story isn't ordered so that the principal meaning is developed (the reader's questions answered in the sequence they will be asked), there's no reason to go on. Find the structure.

- Read for *language*. Make sure each word communicates the meaning of the story. Break the traditions of language only when it is essential to clarify meaning.

20. Write for Yourself

Of course you must listen to editors, to colleagues (especially those who make you want to write when you leave), and to readers. We all need test readers to see if we are communicating and editor-protectors to keep us from playing the unintentional fool, but writing is a lonely business. Ironically, we are motivated as writers by a hunger for applause, for praise, for love, and yet we grow as writers by going our lonely way.

Editors and readers do not know what they want until they read it.

Doris Lessing says, "You have to create your own demand." Exceptional writing cannot be commanded. It has to come from within the writer, surprising the writer as much as it may surprise the reader. Be realistic, do what you have to do to get published, but don't take anyone else—especially a writing coach—too seriously. March to your own command.

EIGHTEEN

REVEALING PEOPLE ON THE PAGE

Our challenge is to make people come alive on the page in realistic dimension. Newswriters have the same challenge as the novelist, biographer, or dramatist: to bring order to disorder, to give fair meaning to apparent meaninglessness, to reveal a sequence of actions and reactions that rarely was apparent at the time they occurred. We must accept the fact that we distort and simplify; our responsibility is to do it fairly, to place the lives of subjects in a significant context, and to reveal them as completely as possible to our readers. The stories that attempt biography in the newspaper usually fall into two categories: the interview and the profile.

The Interview

The interview normally has one principal source, the subject. The purpose of the interview is to allow the reader to hear and see an individual in the news as that person describes the issues from the source's point of view. What the person says is of primary importance, not who he or she is or what he or she is like.

The reader should hear what the subject says and how the subject says it. The interview should reproduce the music of the subject's language, which reveals the person behind the words. The reader should see the subject physically, ideally in actions that reveal the subject to the reader.

The interview may be on a limited topic or range over many subjects, but the story should carry a single dominant impression. Just one? I think so. A well-developed story has texture—there are many things going on within the story—but one theme or meaning should dominate. The story should have a single focus and each element should be connected to and advance that meaning. This dominant impression doesn't need to be simplistic; it can, and should, encompass tension, conflict, and confusion. A story's focus may be on a conflict, a contradiction, or an inaction as well as an action, but the story should give a clear message. Selection is at the center of our art; it is our strength and our weakness.

There should be a clarification and simplification that is fair and in an appropriate context when the story is finished.

The Profile

The profile goes beyond the interview to reveal the subject with more complexity. The subject is *a* source, not *the* source and, in fact, may not even be the principal source.

The reader does not usually see the world from the point of view of the subject (although that *may* be a way to write a profile) but stands back and sees the subject from one perspective or many. The reader is shown the subject from the point of view of others as well as the subject's own point of view; the writer organizes complication and contradiction into a dominant impression that is fair and significant.

The reader hears the subject in the subject's own voice and hears the voices of sources in their own voices. The subject is revealed in significant action. And it all adds up to a single dominant impression that simplifies—fairly, we hope.

We should, through the study of other newspaper interviews and subjects; through reading magazines, biographies, short stories, and novels; through studying plays, movies, and television; through reflecting on our own experience; and through interviewing our colleagues, continue to learn how to make people come alive on the page.

Here are some tricks of the trade I have found helpful:

Preparing for an Interview or Profile

- Write down the five questions the *reader* will ask.

- List as many sources as possible, past and present, friend and enemy, including people who do not know the subject but who are affected by the subject.

- Imagine you are the subject. View the world from the subject's point of view.

- Read the clips but remember you are doing your story. Look for details (chronology and sources) but do not over-react to the stories others have written by following the pack or rebelling against the pack.

Reporting an Interview or Profile

- Pay attention to what is surprising you, to what you are learning that you did not expect.

- Consider the distance you stand from the subject. How much of yourself should you reveal? How empathetic should you be? Be consistent and natural in your style, whether Teddy Bear or Prosecuting Attorney.

- Listen to what the subject and the sources are saying and *how* they are saying it. Try to capture the how as well as the what—the gesture, the actions, the pauses and pacing—so you can re-create that in the writing.

- Observe the subject's world and the subject in that world *before* interviewing the subject if possible.

- Take notes as well as tape, not only to protect yourself if the tape doesn't work but to capture your observations that will not be recorded on the tape. Work to create a natural manner that puts the subject at ease.

- Keep track of lines that are evolving; repeated events, images, or metaphors; and problems or concerns expressed by the subject or those around the subject.

- Interview the subject in conditions in which the subject is comfortable and remember such environments are significant. Or confront the subject in a place where he or she is exposed under stress—the surgeon in the operating room, the surgeon telling the family that the patient has died.

- Observe the subject at work if possible. Note how people react to the subject and how the subject reacts to people.
- Consider three interviews if you have time: one to get to know each other, another to get most of the information, and a third to develop points and resolve inconsistencies.
- Ask the subject to describe himself or herself and the essential work the subject does. Invite the subject to reflect. Many subjects are doers and have not reflected upon their lives as neurotic reporters have.
- Ask the subject and others for additional sources.

Preparing to Write the Interview or Profile

- You may have to type up your notes—I always mean to—but if you do, do not confuse stenography with writing. Step back. Put the notes away. Take out a pad of paper, think about the story. Tell it to yourself or a trusted editor or colleague. What surprised you, what did you learn, what one thing above everything else?
- Give the meaning of the story in one sentence.
- Write the head or the billboard for the story.
- Write fifteen leads, twenty-five, thirty, or fifty (as fast as possible, averaging about three minutes a lead) that will first reveal the direction, pace, and voice of the story and then refine it. The leads you do not use will often be turning points in the story or the end.
- Quickly draft a dozen endings for the story. Pick one.
- List the three to five specific pieces of information that will carry you from the lead to the end.
- Visualize, perhaps even draw, the shape of the story.
- Decide on the length with the editor and then decide how you can work within it. Realize that, indeed, less may be more.

Writing the Interview or Profile

- Write the story fast, in one sitting, so that you can run ahead of the censor, encourage insightful accident, and spin out a coherent tone and sequence.
- Use dialogue as well as quotations.
- Reveal the person physically in significant action.
- Put the subject in a place. Use specific details that reveal the subject.
- Write a lead that helps you and the reader to understand the essential issue of the story.
- Listen for a voice that is consistent and appropriate to the meaning of the story.
- Answer the reader's questions *when* they will be asked.
- Construct the dominant impression using a sequential body of evidence that does not so much tell the reader how to react but invites the reader to react.
- Vary the documentation so that you are using the form of documentation that best supports the point being made.
- Consider anecdotes—little stories with character, action and reaction, dialogue, and setting—that make a significant and fair point. Make sure they advance the meaning of the story.
- Give the reader a trail to follow through the story, such as narrative, chronology, cause and effect, problem and solution, process, or a walk with the subject.
- Do what works for you. If nothing is working, go back and re-create the conditions that worked on a similar story in the past. Remember that we can learn from others, but we have our own working style as well as our own writing style. Keep them evolving.
- Write to reveal the subject to you and then to the reader; write to satisfy yourself, then the reader, and possibly an editor.

NINETEEN

THE CRAFT
OF DESCRIPTION

Too often we think of description as a way to decorate a story when it may be the story. Visualization is a way of thought; we see to understand and the craft of description serves us in many ways.

Description makes the meaning of the story concrete; it makes the story, and its significance, accessible to the reader. Before that stage, the act of writing perceptive description may reveal the importance of the story to the writer. Young children write drawings. They see no difference between writing the drawing and writing the caption or story to go with the drawing. And published writers report that they observe the story with their mind's eye and then record it. That is certainly my experience whether I am writing fiction, poetry, or nonfiction.

Description (accurate, clear, precise, description) reveals the story to the reader. It allows the reader to observe the mayor in action, to observe the process by which a law is passed, or to see the implication of a law on a taxpayer.

Readers deserve more than our opinion of what has happened. Yes, stories written as if they were cleansed of all opinion are just that; the writer's view of what the Massachusetts House, the Red Sox, or the MIT researchers have done. Our "opinion" of what has happened will only be believed if we deliver supporting evidence, and description can be an effective way of providing convincing documentation.

Many stories in a newspaper float like balloons that have escaped from wailing five-year-olds. (That quick descriptive simile may help you to see an idea: stories that have no context. Description may liven up an essay about the craft of description. We can sneak description into our stories with a word, a phrase, a quote, a simile, or a metaphor.) One way to bring the floating story down to earth is with description that puts the story in context. Description makes the medical theory visit the ward and the economic theory man the register in the supermarket check-out lane.

Readers usually need a sense of place to experience and understand the story. They need to ride the subway, to sit with the jury, and to be in the operating room, the laboratory, or the project apartment. The responsible reporter/writer puts the reader there with well-crafted description based on careful, observant reporting.

Often we have to prepare the reader for the story we must deliver, to establish the mood, to set the scene: description again.

Readers want to read about people and description populates the story. The legislature becomes a working collection of individuals, the police become a cop alone on a beat, and taxpayers become a couple with a fixed income and a zooming real estate tax (Can they afford to stay in the home they own?).

Description can add texture and depth to a story, allowing the reader to see significant complexity: The welfare mother has a rented television, a rented VCR, a rented hi-fi, and a video game being purchased on time; the reader is shown these "luxuries" and then the addicts in the project stairwell, the gangs strutting in the yard outside, the thirteen-year-old pimping for his eleven-year-old sister. The reader discovers the "luxuries" are an electronic moat one mother is trying to build around her children so they will never go out to play the project games.

Description is too often considered passive; it can, and should, provide energy and deliver information that drives the story forward.

Techniques of Description

In school description is normally taught in isolation from other forms of writing, as if it were a chunk of prose shoehorned into the text, and this misconception remains in too many writers' skulls. Description can, and should, be woven through the text.

To explore some of the possibilities of description, I am going to take a flat description and show the effects of different descriptive techniques. But do not forget that most effective description is not isolated in this way; it appears where the reader needs to see and can be woven into almost any sentence or paragraph. I am doing this exercise to learn more than teach. Try it yourself to discover and sharpen your writing tools.

The body was found in the kitchen of the Dorchester Street house.

Make a word more active.	**The body was** discovered **in the kitchen of the Dorchester Street house.**
Use a word with a different connotation.	**The body was discovered in the kitchen of the Dorchester Street** *home.*
Add a word or two to make the sentence more descriptive.	**The** *mother's* **body was discovered in the kitchen of the Dorchester Street** *home.*
Add a specific piece of information such as age, title, etcetera.	**The** *twenty-three-year-old* **mother's body was discovered in the kitchen of** *her* **Dorchester Street** *home.*
Add a revealing detail.	**The twenty-three-year-old mother's body was discovered in the kitchen of her Dorchester Street home.** *Hamburg for home-made spaghetti sauce simmered on the stove.*
Give the reader an image.	*Steam still rose from the* **hamburg simmering for home-made spaghetti sauce** *after the* **twenty-three-year-old mother's body was discovered in the kitchen of her Dorchester Street home.**

Move a detail to the beginning or end of the paragraph for emphasis.	*(See previous example.)*
Add a quotation.	*"Maria was always in the kitchen," her mother said, "making home-made bread, listening to other people's problems, doing for the kids, writing her poems at the kitchen table."*
One of the most important techniques of description is to work from or towards a dominant impression.	*The spiral notebook open, the pen uncapped, the last line of poetry half-written, the meat for spaghetti sauce simmering on the stove, the kitchen revealed evidence of an unfinished life.* *or* *The kitchen revealed evidence of an unfinished life: the spiral notebook open, the pen uncapped, the last line of poetry unwritten, the meat for the spaghetti sauce simmering on the stove.*
Use of a phrase to focus the description.	*See an unfinished life above.*
Describing a process is an effective descriptive technique.	*Her mother turned off the stove, capped the pen, read to the unfinished line and closed the notebook.*
Another good way to organize descriptive details is to use a natural order: a walk through, a clock ticking, or the way the eye moves, not left to right but from one item to another in a normal sequence.	*Maria's mother ran right to the kitchen, stopped, looking directly at the police and the reporters, then down to her daughter, to the stove, to the notebook on the table, finally to her daughter again.*

Use another sense than sight whenever possible.

Even after her mother had turned off the stove, the kitchen was filled with the spicy smell of a meal that would never be served.

Most of us describe everything at the same distance when we should use the distance most effective for what we are trying to say and we should remember that readers are familiar with the zoom lens. We can start far away and move in close or reverse the process.

Through the window, it looked like a family kitchen, filled with friends, but inside there was silence and the body of a young mother sprawled, face up, on the floor.

We can describe by comparison or analogy, which is effective if it is accurate *and appropriate,* disastrous if it is not. For example, listen to the presidential candidate or political columnist of your choice using sports and military analogies.

The old car in the driveway had bumper stickers over bumper stickers, each against war, but the scene in the kitchen looked like a clip of a terrorist attack in another country.

Angle of vision is vital in description. The writer's eye organizes the description. The reader should sense where that eye is, be able to see everything that can be seen from that spot, and not see what can't be seen from that spot. The eye will make the reader seasick if it hops around like an amateur video film maker at a wedding. It helps me, if I have problems with angle of vision, to imagine that, like Christopher Isherwood, "I am a camera," and I move around until I find the angle of vision that serves the reader best.

(Look for the camera in the descriptions above: What was the angle of vision? What should it have been?)

From the back door, where her husband and their son came in from day care, the body was hidden, but not the blood.

The front door was open and the front rooms were dark. All the light came from the kitchen where the door was filled by the backs of police overcoats. A dog whimpered from the basement.

Joseph Conrad said that a novel is a series of "scenes of confrontation." I have to remind myself of that powerful statement when writing fiction, but it has significant implications for the nonfiction writer as well. Readers like to read scenes because they "see" and "hear" the interaction of people and because they are not told how to think or feel but are given the room to observe and reflect, to experience the text and respond to it in their way. The scene may be short or long but it is usually built from these elements: *characters* (individual, believable people) who *act and react* to each other through *dialogue* which, as Elizabeth Bowen reminded us, is action; and that action/reaction takes place in a *setting*.

"You can't go in the kitchen, Ma'am."
The detective moved to block the door.

"My daughter called me." Alice Storrs tried to push by the detective.

"When did she call?"

"It was on the answering machine. I came as soon as. . . ."

The mother moved to the left and the detective moved to block her.

"I'm too late."

"I'm sorry."

"He did it, then. We thought he was just talking, you know."

"Who's he?"

(All right, I know, reporters don't usually get there to hear such conversations, but sometimes they do. All I'm trying to do is to demonstrate how a brief scene might work to put the reader there, to make the reader feel and identify with the feelings of the mother and learn how the police discovered the name of the suspect. The lead on a first-day story would not have this scene, but the story might, and the scene certainly might be a sidebar or folo story. We can observe or, with care, reconstruct scenes in the corporate boardroom, in the hospital waiting room, in the locker room— scenes that reveal the story to the reader.

TWENTY

FITTING MORE NEWS INTO LESS SPACE

Through the years writers have stared with horror, looking over the edge, as the news hole has shrunk. Some papers have carried this too far and make across-the-board ultimatums about story length. I think there should be a diversity of lengths but that each story should earn its space. In my own experience, however, shorter is usually better.

Here are some of the problems writers have faced when required to shrink their story length.

I tend to look for the big story in all that I do and then have enormous problems wrestling it down to newspaper size. Any advice?

- Look for the single, most revealing anecdote, quote, statistic, detail, or fact. Focus in close.

- Recognize that each story must have one dominant message. Kurt Vonnegut once said, "Don't put anything in a story that does not reveal character or advance the action." That's superb fiction-writing advice that can, and should, be applied to our trade. Every thing in the story should move the story forward toward its final meaning.

- Steinbeck put on a 3-by-5 card a sentence or two that encapsulated the meaning of each book he was writing. Try that. I've found it invaluable.

- Each story should answer the reader's questions. Usually there are four or five questions the reader must have answered. Ask them, and answer them.

- Draft a dozen leads, or two dozen. Just the first line or so. Do it quickly—a matter of minutes for each one—until you find the lead that focuses the story. Then develop that lead.

- Outline. Make a note of the lead, then the ending. Put down the three to five main points in between and then number them so that they take you from the lead to the end.

- Decide on the form of the story. It may be inverted pyramid, narrative, profile, problem/solution, exposé, analysis, question and answer, scene and exposition, walk through, or whatever; but each form has its own discipline, qualities that drive it forward and those that get in the way.

- Choose the voice. Each story has its voice, that speaking quality of style, tone, and tempo that holds the story together. Knowing (naming and testing) the voice is a great help in selecting what belongs in the story and what should be left out.

- Write the first draft fast without your notes. What you remember will probably be what you should remember, and what is forgotten probably should be forgotten. And you will, of course, check your notes after you finish the draft to make sure that's true.

- Write for one reader. Imagine a person you know and write to that person. A story that includes too much and lacks focus is often written to satisfy the chorus of editors and censors who haunt us all.

How do you write the forty-to-fifty-line story with humor or punch?

Accept limitation as an artistic challenge. Brevity can clarify and concentrate the mind the way combat or being rolled into an operating room can do. All art involves restrictions, and the size of a canvas, the duration of a symphony, and the length of a story are essential parts of the artistic process.

Art is also a matter of selection. The trick in the short article is to select the essential part of the story and then to develop it fully.

Most writers, when ordered to write short, make the mistake of writing the garbage compactor story, compressing everything that is in the notebook into a hard, indigestible pellet of news. There were few good things I learned at *Time,* but I did see selection and development in a different way than I had before I went there.

Stories of any length should have one dominant meaning. Effective short stories *must* have one dominant meaning. Everything in the story should lead toward or away from that meaning. The pace of the story, its form, its order, and its tone should all support that single meaning. And the story should be developed with all the information to satisfy the reader and to give the story appropriate texture.

Too many long stories are filled with information that the reporter includes in case someone (usually an editor) says, why didn't you include x, y, or z? The brief story requires hard decisions and trust. Interesting information will be left out. There is no way that you can write a short save-your-ass story. Such stories require team work between writer and editor. But the result is worth the effort. Most stories get better as they get shorter.

What are some tips for keeping any story to eighty lines . . . or, how to write anything in eighty lines?

- Write the ending first so that you have a clear sense of direction as you write the draft.

- Draft ten, fifteen, twenty leads or first sentences taking only three minutes or less for each one.

- Write a headline or a billboard that will concentrate the focus of the story.

- Ask yourself the one essential question the reader will ask. Answer it.

- Write fast without your notes, remembering what you should remember, forgetting what should be forgotten.

- Make a list of all the interesting information, all the potential stories in the story that do not advance the dominant message to the reader. Leave them all out.

TWENTY ONE

ANALYSIS OF A TOM ASHBROOK STORY

It is possible to report a story before it occurs. Tom Ashbrook gathered the background information for this story and when a raid came he was ready and pounced.

GOODWINS MILLS, Maine—The cops came early and they got it all: heaps and bundles and lush green acres of prime Maine reefer, the best darn marijuana crop that Billy Carvell had ever seen.

This is a good example of vigorous lead writing with the added touch of hinting at the voice appropriate to the locale of the story. Too much would be hokey; the right amount adds appropriate liveliness to a story that would usually be greeted with a loud ho-hum.

It was hanging from the barn rafters. It was leaping up ten feet behind the brush and cedars. It was tied down bushy and flat to hide between the corn rows and growing like crazy a stone's throw from the Hebron Community Church.

Notice how active this description is: hanging, leaping, hiding, growing. Then at the point in the paragraph of most emphasis, the end, we have the church.

But mentioning the church has a purpose, it demonstrates the point of the story that pot is being grown in the rural heartland of America,

Republican, church-going, Norman Rockwell country. Too often we have nice touches that do nothing to advance the meaning of the story.

From the road, you never would have guessed it. The Carvell farm looks straight off a Maine travel poster. A red and white barn on a country road. A "pick your own" tomato patch every summer. Pumpkin on the lawn every fall.

Again, this paragraph puts the story in a context and reinforces the meaning being developed.

But when York County police moved in on the homestead Monday morning, they found more than $1 million worth of marijuana, about two hundred pounds cut and dried and ready to go, plus 1,300 thriving plants.

I don't like the term "delayed lead" because I think that Ashbrook's lead contained the news, but by the third or fourth paragraph of a story that depends on description and tone, the reader needs some hard facts. Here they are delivered in hard-edged specifics.

"If you know anything about marijuana, you'd be impressed with this," said one detective with grudging admiration after the raid, handling a thick cluster of succulent buds. "This is as good as it gets."

A nice time for a quote, an attribution, another authority than the reporter speaking. There's a nice bit of action woven into the attribution as well.

Each paragraph—each sentence, each phrase, each word—should drive the story forward. The reader should receive a delivery of information that will satisfy the reader's hunger for information and increase the reader's appetite for more information.

Out on bail, Tuesday, alleged pot farmer William H. Carvell, 43, was more taciturn:

I'm not sure I understand who he is more taciturn than or even if that's the right word, but I need the facts in the paragraph and I like the way the quotation is set up.

"I'm just a country farmer who found out there was more money in pot than in corn," he said.

The effective writer anticipates the reader's questions and answers them. The reader asks how a Maine farmer would get in the pot trade. Ashbrook lets the farmer answer.

Indeed. And not only for Billy Carvell.

An important transition and made clear enough so that the reader sees the turn in the road. Ashbrook's reader will not get lost, the writer is unobtrusively but effectively in charge.

It is harvest time in the world's premier marijuana patch, the United States of America.

Just about the time the reader is getting tired of the story, the author raises the ante. It's a new game. I'd better stay in and read on.

Cocaine may grab the big headlines these days. Crack may send cities into turmoil. But deep in the coke trade's shadow, marijuana—the dowdy green matron of the drug scene—has become one of the largest cash crops in the United States. And America has earned a dubious distinction as home to the cream of world marijuana production.

Anticipation again. The reader's going to begin saying, so what? What about coke, what about crack? Ashbrook puts the pot trade into context and tells the reader how important this story is.

As recently as 1980, by federal estimates, just 7 percent of available pot in America was domestically produced. The vast majority and the best quality of marijuana came from Mexico, Colombia, the Caribbean and Southeast Asia.

You don't believe me? Well, step back a minute and let me give you a bit of history.

But by last year, America's homegrown portion of pot had nearly quadrupled, to account for 25 percent or more of the country's available marijuana. And the quality crown, judged on potency, had come home. "Americans now grow the best pot in the world," says Brian Murphy, a staff member at the National Organization for the Reform of Marijuana Laws, in Washington. "It's the Dom Perignon of the marijuana industry."

The writer should never forget that readers want to be informed. Readers want the Globe to make them authorities; they want to be able to tell their co-workers, their neighbors, and their families something new. Ashbrook gives them surprising information they can use to surprise the people around them.

Predicting that the United States might become a net exporter of marijuana in the 1990s, exasperated federal law officials agree.

And listen to this.

". . . produce the best"

"We can grow it here," says Jack Short, acting chief of the federal Drug Enforcement Agency's marijuana section, "and we can produce the best."

And this.

Both these facts are well known to a growing circle of American pot producers. Estimates of the domestic pot crop's value now range from

Ashbrook wraps up the information he has delivered above and makes the transition back to who's growing it. By using the word moonshine he

$10 billion to $30 billion. From cash-strapped farmers to highly organized criminal syndicates, the lucrative production of America's new moonshine has proven an irresistible lure.

With domestic marijuana production reaching unprecedented levels, the summer has produced a raft of eye-opening pot tales. A sampling:

• In Tucson, a Mecca for allergy sufferers where marijuana can not grow without careful cultivation, officials reported last month that pot pollen led all others in Tucson's daily pollen count, outranking Bermuda grass, salt cedar and ragweed. "I guess we aren't winning," said a local police officer. "We never do."

• In Fort Benton, Mont., a prominent farming family raised and sold more than $400,000 worth of marijuana in a failed attempt to save the farm from foreclosure. "It was either do this and save the ranch or there wasn't going to be any ranch," said a son-in-law.

• In Akron, Ohio, a major University of Akron area landlord was arrested this month after police shut down a sophisticated underground pot production chamber. Police said Albert Thrower owned 30 cars, 300 college rental properties, an air-

gives the story an appropriate historical perspective, harkening back to another time when rural America was engaged in illicit activity.

Once more, he lets the reader in on what he is doing—"Hey, come over here and lookit this!"

The writer uses an interesting variety of anecdotes.
*   Pot pollen; that's amazing, says the reader.*

An echo of what the Maine farmer said. His was not an isolated case.

A pet hate of mine is to use area in this way. GRRRRR.
*   But we have another form of pot production and, because the writer has earned our trust, we believe it is typical of a larger problem.*

plane, six legal businesses—and a marijuana goldmine concealed behind a trapdoor in his barn floor.

"If we didn't have such a big coke problem, we would be taking better care of our marijuana problem," said the DEA's Short, calling the 7.4 million pot plants eradicated last year only a fraction of the total crop. "The vast majority of our resources go to cocaine."

By now the reader's asking, why is something not being done about this problem? Again, Ashbrook anticipates the reader's questions when they will be asked, which is a matter of timing and pacing.

Potent pot

The careful grooming of prime strains and new hybrids has produced a level of pot potency largely unknown in the 1960s, when a rebellious generation of baby boom Americans turned on to cannabis. Recent crops of American pot have yielded record-breaking levels of tetrahydrocannabinol, or THC, the psycho-active chemical in marijuana.

Once more, the writer recognizes when the reader will grow tired of the story and raises the ante: The new U.S. pot is especially powerful.

He also puts this in historical perspective by weaving in a reference to the 60s.

Note how quickly he explains a technical name. All the way through he uses language in such a way that the pot sophisticate and ignorant old-timer like myself can understand the story.

In 1986, the average THC content in sensimilla pot seized by US enforcement agencies was 8.5 percent, almost triple what was once the norm and twice the potency of pot coming in from Mexico and Colombia. Symbolic of pot's new

Good details with a lively touch at the end of the paragraph that picks the reader up and pushes him or her toward the next paragraph.

hierarchy, Colombians have recently been reported smoking American marijuana on the streets of Bogota.

The stabilization of potent hybrids has brought a new sophistication to pot shopping. The talk of marijuana connoisseurs has begun to sound like the airy blurbs in a Macy's wine catalogue.

Effective bit of lively language.

Ed Rosenthal, a columnist for High Times magazine, recently described current favorites among premium pots in an interview:

Now the writer is going to document what he just said.

On Afghani Durban—"A dense, fragrant smoke. Not sweet, more musky. It has a very soaring high. It's light."
    On Skunk No. 1—"An odor a lot like skunk, but a very smooth taste, a very up high. Heavy yielding."

Amusing examples, but they aren't used just to entertain; they testify to the popularity of pot in a time when coke, crack, etcetera dominate the news, and they speak to the potency of the present marijuana, a major point in the story.

On Northern Lights—"Perhaps the most potent pot there is. An Afghani sativa. Very strong, but lacks personality. Like vodka. Usually crossed with something to give it more character."

It always helps to allow the reader to hear other voices within the story, especially when the voice supports a major thesis of the article as this voice does. Ashbrook gets out of the way and let's this authority speak.

And the price? Good grades run from $150 to $300 per ounce and up across the country, with Boston-area smokers of the illegal weed paying at the high end.

Put the reader's question right in the story. The answer supports the reason why so much is grown. It is a cash crop.

May cost more than money

Officials warn that pot smoking—especially of America's potent new product—can cost a user more than money.

We've been having fun. It all seems silly and harmless. So the writer turns the story level up again. This transition paragraph announces to the reader that important information is on the way. You'd better keep reading.

A recent survey of more than 1,000 emergency patients at Maryland hospitals' shock/trauma units found that 35 percent had used marijuana within four hours of the injury that landed them in the emergency ward. Thirty-three percent had used alcohol. Sixteen percent had used both.

Good, solid, hard news.

"The unspoken fact of American life is that marijuana kills," says Robert S. Wiener, a spokesman for the House Select Committee on Narcotics. "The reality is that it's very, very harmful."

He puts that limited study in a broader context.

Law enforcement officials say that the trend in recent years has been toward scattered cultivation in many small, less easily detected plots and toward indoor growing under artificial light.

Now the story is going to achieve closure. It won't just drift off, but will echo the beginning so that the reader will see the original pot raid from a new and significant perspective.

Oregon, California and Hawaii usually lead in pot production. Massachusetts ranked 34th among the 50 states in a 1987 National Organization for the Reform of Mar-

Authoritative details with a nice kicker at the end: bat guano, indeed.

ijuana Laws survey of marijuana crops. But indoor production knows no bounds, with national trade magazines hawking everything from seeds and growing kits to Kentucky bat guano fertilizer.

National parks a favorite

Other favorite production spots for pot farmers weary of having their own land seized in an arrest are US national parks and forests. The National Forest Service estimates that last year alone it destroyed $1 billion worth of marijuana on public lands, and it found less than half of what was there.

Another unexpected site.

In York County, Maine, detective Michael McAlevey estimates that even with the big bust of Billy Carvell this week, his department is detecting only 10 percent of the marijuana grown in Maine's southernmost county.

Now we return to York County, after having seen the dimensions and significance of the problem.

"We have hearsay that there are doctors out there doing it, lawyers doing it, businessmen doing it," said McAlevey, who grew up a mile down the road from the Carvell farm and went to school with Billy.

"Plus, there's a Yankee attitude that you mind your own business—that what somebody else is doing behind their barn is their own business."

And it isn't just the farmers.

Nice touch that increases his stature as an authority. He's a native who knows what's going on.

Out along the Maine backroads, where handwritten signs advertise the legal bounty of the land—sod, rabbits, hardy mums—neighbors said knowingly that Billy Carvell's bust was not the end of the local harvest of moonshine marijuana.

Back to Norman Rockwell country. This story is shaped like a diamond. Many of us, myself included, think it can be helpful to visualize the shape of a story. I even draw such shapes in planning a complex story, something that Updike has done for some of his novels. Ashbrook's story starts with a specific raid on a specific farm, then shows the significance in many ways.

He puts it in several economic perspectives, even in a perspective of world trade. He introduces us to the new and powerful pot, considers law enforcement problems, points out the health dangers involved, and then, once we have the information we need to understand the significance of what Billy Carvell was doing on his farm, brings us right back there.

"Let's put it this way," said one, stuffing a wad of tobacco into his cheek and glancing into the woods. "There's a lot more out there to be picked."

TWENTY TWO

ANALYSIS OF TWO DAVID ARNOLD STORIES

David Arnold works general assignment, ready to handle any story that breaks. He is versatile and he is good. Here I put the magnifying glass on two of his stories so that I, and you, may learn.

On February 7, 1990, Arnold wrote a story that began:

The year Paul Tucker the football player made all–New England tackle was the year Paul Tucker the art student stood before one of a series of paintings by Claude Monet and wondered: "Wouldn't it be nice to reunite them someday."

This could have been a puff piece on a museum, a ho-hum opening, but Arnold gets a person in the lead and sets up dramatic tension: The student has a dream.

Tucker has done just that. His "Monet in the '90s" exhibition of series paintings, opening today at the Museum of Fine Arts, is one of the most significant compilations of

The dream is fulfilled, but it wasn't easy. Arnold fills his story with anecdotes, quotes from Tucker and others, and specific information about the problems of building such

French Impressionist work ever assembled, according to art historians.

Some of his quests have been less successful. Take the search for one of Monet's 10 Creuse Valley paintings. It started four years ago with the incomplete records of a London auction house as Tucker attempted to trace the painting's whereabouts. Partial records sent him to a modest home outside Paris and a Madame Y, who sent him back to London— and then to a secretary for Elizabeth Taylor. Taylor, sources recalled, had purchased the painting.

Tucker, governed by tools of his trade he calls "The 3 F's": Federal Express, FAXes, and "Fones," finally reached Taylor at her home outside Los Angeles via a string of acquaintances. Yes, she would loan her Monet.

Quickly, Tucker located a photographer in Los Angeles and dispatched him to Taylor's home so the painting could be photographed for the book, already at the printer, that accompanies the exhibit. Three days later, four years into the search, the photographer's 8-by-10 transparency arrived in Tucker's office.

an exhibition. He closes his piece with some reverse tension, a hunt that hasn't worked out—yet. Note the easy way Arnold uses narrative.

And he weaves in details of Tucker's trade.

He paces the story well.

Arnold often combines longer paragraphs or sentences with short ones for emphasis as he does here.

It was the wrong Monet.

"Nice picture, though," Tucker noted. But it was inappropriate for the series theme of the exhibit.

Tucker continues to look for the missing Creuse Valley canvas. He's been back to Paris, three weeks ago at Madame Y's door once again, and continues to chase down new leads in hopes of making the Chicago opening in May, or perhaps even the latter part of the Boston show.

"I'm not giving up," he said, his teeth seemingly ever so slightly clenched.

Reading that story I appreciate the reporting that went into it, the asking of the right questions, the seeking and reseeking of the specific, revealing detail. Arnold's reporter eye (and ear) is apparent in a story that appeared two days later. This story would have been kissed off by many journalists. It isn't a *serious* story. But it is a story that made page one more lively and was read, I suspect, by more readers than most serious stories that day.

> Lisa Lyles had researched the challenge and knew the demands. So she planned and trained—swimming laps for aerobic capacity and practicing yoga for mind control.
>
> But in the end it was a swatch of tacky cloth applied to the fingers that gave this compact, 130-pound Melrose resident the racer's edge yesterday.
>
> Sticky-fingered Lyles, with an ear for expensive opera, was able to snag 60 compact discs worth $2,054 during a two-minute dash through the aisles of Tower Records.

Again the story is packed with specifics. On February 19, 1990, in the Health and Science section, David Arnold pops up with a story about poverty in the 1800s that begins:

Bailey Taft was a stone mason from Uxbridge 160 years ago, a man in the prime of life but so desperate for funds that he mortgaged his hand-hewn rocks for a loan he couldn't repay. In a subsequent loan, he lost the tools of his trade.

Not even the labor of his five daughters in a nearby textile mill could keep Taft from landing in the local poorhouse shortly before he died in 1871.

Arnold's story goes on to report some surprising discoveries about poverty in the last century. It was, however, in the February 11, 1990, *Globe* that David Arnold wrote a story in which he was both reporter and participant.

FERGUSON, British Columbia— We descend pitch after pitch, our turns blasting waist-deep powder snow overhead in terrain so wild and steep that our guide calls it "just this side of Tiger Country."

This is no delayed lead. Arnold puts us right on the slope with him.

Up here, they call unskiable terrain Tiger Country.

Now he defines that term and emphasizes it as he does.

But we are chomping at its edges, the fastest 10 of 44 skiers who had come to heli-ski a new wilderness pocket of the Canadian Rockies recently opened by Canadian Mountain Holidays. In our hearts we are an invincible platoon, leaping 15-foot cliffs with a yelp and then plummeting thousands of vertical feet with hardly a stop.

A neat context paragraph (nut graf, billboard, who ha, pick your own jargon) that locates the story. Note, however, that he includes their feelings in the last half of the paragraph, foreshadowing what is coming.

At the end of the day, one of us would be dead.

Bang! Dependent clause and straightforward sentence. Here is another case of using a shift from longer paragraph to short for emphasis.

Eric King, a 45-year-old resident of Santa Monica, Calif., died alone 12 days ago on a steep slope of a mountain called Hanging Gardens. He had more than 3 million vertical feet of heli-skiing to his record, an accumulation of wilderness skiing shared by perhaps two dozen Canadian Mountain Holiday veterans.

Now we need exposition and we get it. Arnold is answering the reader's questions as they are asked: "Who died? What happened? How come? Who was he?"

"I like to ski fast, and I hate being last," he liked to say.

Again a short paragraph to emphasize the victim's attitude toward dangerous skiing.

His death was particular to this environment where seemingly bottomless power creates wind-blown hollows around tree trunks that can snare you like quicksand. King fell backwards into a hollow and suffocated, drowning in the powder snow we had come to dance in.

Now we get the technical details explained in clear terms.

. . . Here, the risk of avalanche is minimal, our guide, Danny Stoffel, tells us, just before the ground starts to move.

Later in the story Arnold brings himself into the experience. It documents the dangers they would face and their mixture of fear and innocence that was swinging towards fear. The reader is placed within the experience and this foreshadows the ending of the story. Notice how he sets up the tension between what they are told and what happens.

I hear the avalanche before I see it, a whoosh of snow, like sand from a dump truck.

It always helps when you can use another sense, in this case hearing.

"Avalanche!" shouts Jim Wolff, an emergency room physician at the Emerson Hospital in Concord. I'm close by, as is Peter Swift, an oncologist from Burlington, VT.

The slide is perhaps 80 feet wide and carries 300 feet downhill, leaving a fracture wall at its top about one foot high. Wolff's skis have cut the snow free; it misses me by feet but slips Swift on the opposite side. The boiling snow spits one of his skis 20 feet high, sending it shimmying like a hooked marlin. The ski knifes back into the snow and disappears.

Arnold works in names, etcetera with grace and clearly describes what is happening.

Seconds later, the world is quiet except for bursts of muffled voices in the falling snow. Swift is uninjured but visibly shaken: as is Wolff. Our guide, waiting for us below at the helicopter pickup site, had not seen the incident but seems awfully quick at assessing it as "sloughing." We should expect five, maybe six a day when it snows this hard, Stoffel says.

"Just ski them out on top," he says.

And hearing is used again: quiet.

Easy to say.

Now a nice touch of humor. And the tone is right for the kind of people doing this skiing.

In the woods, it is hard to ski beside buddies. And they detract from the freedom we are here to celebrate in a world where we can descend

Arnold weaves in a quiet scene playing dominos with Eric King that allows him to let you know the man who will die, and later he takes us

seemingly vertical pitches as the powder brakes our speed. This is freefall in a dream, cliffs are followed by pillow-soft landings, the experience is narcotic.

Skiing the trees requires constant vigilance, charting the course as if steering through shoals with the throttle up. Can I make that slot? Is there room for two turns? Small clearing to the right . . . better line here, and time for nice turns . . . how many is there room for? Can't see a thing for a few turns, so much snow is flying overhead. Ouch, my legs hurt. But here comes a jump— so gentle. Elbows up, now tight trees ahead . . . I smell of balsam.

. . . Now we leap frog each other, one person always close behind the other, partners sharing the untracked snow. I will never know for sure if, midway down a tree-studded ridge called Hot Chili, this new buddy system saved my life. My partner is Ed Swift, a Carlisle resident, a reporter for Sports Illustrated, and no relation to my previous buddy Peter. My confidence is gone; I have become keenly aware of my feet, which are all over the place and are now leading me into a tree well.

I fall facing up, my feet caught in a web of branches, my head under a veil of snow so translucent the air

inside the act of skiing with a brilliant action description. Observe how he builds it up and increases the fragments, the bursts of language, that are appropriate to the way the skier would think at that time. Arnold makes us experience the story as much as he can.

That wonderful touch, using another sense: "I smell of balsam."

Arnold describes the search for King, the result, and what follows in a disciplined manner that is more moving than melodrama. He documents the changed mood of the group and the more disciplined control exerted on the group. And then he takes us back out on the slope with him.

We are prepared for this surprise. Arnold will fall as King did.

seems just inches beyond. The first split second passes smoothly—I think: drop the ski poles, clear the snow, stay calm. But the snow doesn't clear.

The more I wipe the more snow falls in. My lungs are aching now—I had been panting hard going into this fall. Now I flail. So this is panic. Just a precious few inches to air, but I can't rise up. My arms are useless, nothing to push on. No control, lungs exploding. And then there's Swift's hand, clearing the snow from my face. "You seem to be somewhat covered up," Swift says.

He says I was close to the surface, I was just about clear of it and that I hadn't really needed his help.

Effective narrative pacing with revealing details.

I'll make a note of that, Ed.

Again, the touch of macho humor.

I quit for the day and later wonder: had King had a helping hand, would he be alive?

And now a more serious reflection.

By week's end, we have had more snow than guides recall ever falling in these mountains. We have had shoulder-deep powder. We have felt unprecedented exhilaration, shock, fear, and camaraderie. We have had death. I arrived cavalier about the trouble my ability might lead me into, I leave with realigned priorities. My family calls. I leave lucky.

Note the tension within his summary, the good and the bad.

Arnold goes on for a couple of short paragraphs but the story, for me, is over here. In each of these stories, Arnold demonstrates what the good reporter who has command of news style can do to reveal a world to the reader.

TWENTY THREE

Interview:
DAVID ARNOLD

David describes his indirect career line that made him a *Globe* writer:

I was graduated from Harvard in 1971, where I majored in photography, and I don't recall writing a paper after freshman year, such were the demands of a grade-yourself Ivy education in the late 1960s. I earned a Master's Degree in 1976 in design and photography at Yale, then worked as designer/photographer for an architectural firm in Cambridge and then at WGBH television and radio before starting my own design studio. My freelance clients included the Globe, which offered me a full-time design position in 1978 too tasty for a starving entrepreneur to refuse.

I have, from the beginning, been impressed by David's eye and ear and how he has grown until he is one of the most proficient and versatile writers on the *Globe*, ranging, almost daily it seems, between hard news and features.

Your stories are full of powerful images and significant details. I imagine that comes in part from your experience as an artist/designer. Will you talk about what role your background in art plays in your work as a reporter and writer?

When I think I'm a keen observer because of the art background, I discover I've just forgotten whether the guy I interviewed had a beard or moustache, and I end up grabbing a wet photograph from the photo lab to finish the story.

So I'm not sure where the art fits in, although I do catch myself staring at colors, textures, or the lines of facial profiles while I report. I'm a firm believer that I can bring the reader closer by subtly prodding at stimuli that might reach the nose, taste buds, ears, and eyes.

I honestly think theater would be wonderful training for journalism. So much of what we repackage for the reader condenses and distills characters, action, and drama, much as the playwright or screenwriter might do.

Because I still lay out and art direct the stories I write for sports, I sometimes work totally backwards and capitalize on the control.

The normal sequence is to report a story, then write and deliver it to an editor; then a designer chooses the appropriate artwork and fits the story to the available space on the page. I work in reverse.

First (sometimes before I report), I sketch a layout—a storybook, for example—on the pad of tracing paper I keep on my desk. I sketch hits on a tone I may have been unable to articulate. For instance, the storybook format may lead to a fairy tale tone that delivers color and playfulness to the project I never would have envisioned had the process begun with words alone.

Design was a mission because I had been trained for it. It said, "You shalt not fail it because you have invested mightily in it."

But journalism is a grand experiment. It says, "Hey, have fun." I think I make a lot of editors nervous.

Why did you switch from design to writing?

I returned to a Greek island ten years after spending a summer farming there to observe and photograph some pretty drastic changes that had settled in. Wealthy Germans had decided the island made a terrific nudist hideaway. The villagers, who had been devoutly religious, sold their scruples to the tourists.

Mike Janeway, then editor of the *Sunday Magazine,* needed a story fast and suggested I write up the trip. I whimpered about how a high school teacher had told me English must have been my second language. Besides, I couldn't spell. Janeway said: Just show me your observations. I'll worry about the spelling.

So I wrote just as fast as possible. I had nothing to lose. In the end,

Janeway got his story and I got the writing lesson of my life: Writing has more to do with an ability to observe than to spell. I don't think I've ever written a piece that was quite so fresh and uninhibited.

What were the most important things you had to learn?

Not to overwrite, not to spend three paragraphs describing the clash of plaids in the living room decor.

How did you learn that?

I learned by trial and error. I must be one of the few staffers in *Globe* history who has had to correct his own correction. You don't do this more than once.

Who helped you to learn and how did they help?

Alas, the now-departed writing coaches, first Alan Richman, then Bill Miller. They were a constant resource, another ear, impartial observers, and always on my side.

I get very nervous when stories squirt out of the sausage machine here with hardly an editing change. And I'm kidding myself if I believe the prose is impeccable. The truth is that no one has the time to do more than tinker with the writing because, justly, their job is first to get it right and get it clear.

What do you know now that you wish you had known then?

You can take chances, strive for similes and metaphors, be creative, dare to characterize.

Take one of the most boring stories in the newsroom—the day-after-bad-weather-story—and do something different with it: Go sledding in the new snow, join a plowing crew, call Tromso, Norway, and find out just how bad a day folks north of the Arctic Circle had. If the story bombs, at least you won't be asked to do another one for a while.

You go to Russian missile cities, to the Canadian Rockies, to Central American reefs, through the sound barrier in an F-18 jet, and then do quick, daily, general assignment stories. Will you talk a bit about the advantages and disadvantages of each type of assignment?

I think general assignment is the most versatile, stimulating reporting slot on the paper—providing there's opportunity occasionally to wander into other departments for a change of pace. The people I meet on the street in GA usually are under tremendous stress; they teach me daily about myself and perhaps will be role models should fate deal me a bad hand. I don't understand the stigma GA has around here. It's the only position that allows a reporter to write his or her own ticket.

The daily hits obviously facilitate the writing of the longer pieces. I particularly enjoy breaking the unwritten journalism rule that says: Write it immediately after you report it. The *Adventure in Travel* magazine sometimes works a year in advance. If I'm lucky enough to sell it a story, I separate the reporting from the writing by months. This way I'm able to go powder-snow skiing in the summer and kayaking in the winter. I'd like to think a sense of yearning creeps into the writing that enriches the piece.

I've noticed you laughing while you seem to be writing and simultaneously listening to someone on your telephone headphones. What's going on?

Telephone headphones are a terrific editor-avoidance mechanism. I wear them whether I'm on the telephone or not. I laugh when I write sometimes, not because I think I'm the next James Thurber, but because when I go fast enough, the words take me unintended places. The twists can be funny and are almost always worth polishing.

What is your writing process when you do a quick hit and are on deadline? What tricks of the trade do you use?

Never look at notes. Draft first and quote from best representatives of involved parties by fourth or fifth paragraph. The easiest kicker is a quote. Be aware of my own prejudices, and give the last word to the side I personally disagree with.

Is your writing process different when you have more time? What are the significant differences in how you work? What tricks of the trade do you find helpful on those stories?

Take the story down to the back room in the library and read it aloud. I also give it to Dave Morrow, to my mind the writer's editor most accessible on the News Desk. Morrow thinks nothing of proposing an entirely different lead and then working it with me until we decide it's good or terrible. Kathy Everly in Science and Health also has an excellent eye, although she's smarter at avoiding work than Morrow. She doesn't rewrite, she just notes in boldface: "Doesn't work for me here, Babe."

Your endings are unusually good as well. Will you say something about how you work on endings? What do you look for as an effective ending?

If the story is not controversial, I allow my own voice to creep into the ending to personalize it. Joe Kahn in Living does this with diligence.

Do you have any rules or principles you try to follow when writing?

Odd how the following rules have stuck. They could be argued to oblivion, but for me they work.

The first three are from Al Richman:

- There's always a story there somewhere.

- If you need to explain the humor, forget it.

- If the story's good, don't let the writing interfere.

Others are:

- Try for an action verb in the first sentence.

- Don't lead with a subordinate clause.

- Don't lead with a quote.

- If the story's about an individual, get the name in the first paragraph.

- You haven't got a newspaper story if the reader can't use the information.

- Don't end your best quotes with an attribution (put it within the quote, set off with commas).

- A feature about people needs descriptive detail about the people, which takes work. Reference to blonde hair is almost always sexist. The hands (actions, color, condition) can usually give a reader telling detail, as can the knickknacks on living room mantles. Eyes have texture; eye contact is another descriptive tool. But mention of high cheek bones only proves you wasted too much time reading Ian Fleming.

- A story proposed by an editor should be championed by the editor.

- Judge your writing for fairness by whether or not you're willing to send the person you're worried about a clip.

How can an editor help you? How can an editor hinder?

For every time an editor burns me by making phrasing more clunky to my ear, she or he saves me tenfold with points of accuracy.

What advice do you have for young reporters?

Stretch and let the editor rein you in. One of my best experiments was a Christmas story where I followed undercover cops nabbing pickpockets on the subway.

My worst experiment came with some local, seemingly minor flooding. I decided to chart the city's history by "reading" the layers of strata exposed downtown as work crews excavated for pipe damage. Then I discovered some residents had suffered serious property damage. You can't mix cuteness with even minor suffering. It was twenty minutes before deadline and John Burke hadn't had time to rein me in. We ran a wire story. Burke wasn't pleased.

Are there books or writers you would recommend that we read to learn to write more effectively?

Almost any good children's book. I recommend them not because I've read all the literary masterpieces and have worked my way into the library toddler wing. It's because, with two youngsters at home, I don't have time to read anything else. The experience has been an eye opener. Childrens' books often have complex themes, yet the writing is clear and condensed, the vocabulary elementary, the alliteration and rhythms of the words and phrasing playful and always audible, and the humor very funny.

It seems the essence of voice in these books is what's left out, not what's written. So I recommend *Mr. Popper's Penguins* by Florence and Richard Atwater, *Charlotte's Web* by E. B. White, *Amos and Boris* by William Steig, and *One Morning in Maine* by Robert McClosky. Look at it this way: You'll have four books under your belt in one sitting, with time to spare.

TWENTY FOUR

Interview:
RENEE GRAHAM

I talked to Renee Graham soon after she arrived at the *Globe* and was immediately impressed by her attitude and her talent. Again and again I am impressed by her stories.

She majored in newspaper journalism at Syracuse University, graduating in 1984. She worked as an intern for the *Syracuse Herald-Journal* during her senior year and stayed on for two years after college. Desperate for a warmer climate, Graham moved south and worked at the *Miami Herald* for two years as a general assignment reporter, then as the social services reporter. She has been at the *Globe* since March 1988 and is now a member of the Living staff.

How do you prepare for an interview?

It's always annoyed me when some talk-show host or interviewer says, "Well, I haven't read your book, but I've heard . . ." My interest usually fades at that point because I don't think the interviewer is properly equipped. You have to do your homework. You have to know your topic and subject, otherwise you stumble through the interview and never really accomplish what you want to do. Before an interview, I read up on a subject as much as possible. I use back clips, magazine articles, or even transcripts from news shows such as "60 Minutes" and "20/20," if available. I don't believe you can overprepare for an interview. Each bit of background information helps you ask better questions. I also think it impresses your subject if you walk into their home or office with some basic knowledge of their topic or situation.

Do you have any special techniques for telephone interviews?

Obviously, you miss a lot with telephone interviews and it's difficult to put a person immediately at ease since they can't see you; however, that can work to your advantage. When I was in college I worked for a crisis hotline and it never ceased to amaze me how open people would be with someone they couldn't see. Some people seem to find it easier to be interviewed over the telephone.

Do you have any special techniques for face-to-face interviews?

I try to maintain eye contact and keep my own fidgeting to a minimum. It's distracting if the interviewer is rattling papers, crossing and uncrossing his or her legs, playing with loose threads, or staring out the window. If someone has taken the time to talk with me, the least I can do is act like I'm giving them my undivided attention.

How do you get people to answer questions they don't want to answer?

My techniques vary depending on the person. Most of the time, it's give-and-take. I let them talk about something they want to talk about, then I ask them the hard questions. Sometimes, if the person is particularly skittish, I'll ask a tough question right off. That way they think the worst is over and the rest of the interview will be a breeze. If necessary, I'll bury parts of difficult questions in other questions.

How do you collect the revealing details that make your stories clear and lively? What do you look for when reporting a story?

I try to pay special attention to small details: mannerisms, vocal inflections, pauses in speech, and so on. I also look for other revealing things: pictures, wall hangings, anything that can tell a little bit more about a person or topic.

Some writers say they have had a breakthrough piece that has given them confidence. Do you have such a piece. What was it? What was the breakthrough?

I see my magazine story on the teen-age father as my "breakthrough" piece. I'd never written a magazine story before and was quite excited by the opportunity to try something new. The magazine format allowed me to lay aside some of the tenets of newswriting. I could use large chunks of narrative or dialogue in ways that few news editors would allow. I didn't have to worry about a nut graf in the first ten lines. As a writer, I found the experience exhilarating and liberating.

When you have a complicated story do you have any techniques that help you understand and communicate it?

When I'm writing complicated stories, I make sure I ask the simple questions, the types of questions the average *Globe* reader might have. I don't approach stories merely as a newspaper writer, but as a newspaper reader, always keeping in mind small questions that sometimes go unanswered in complicated stories.

I believe you have done other kinds of writing. What were they? How do they help your newswriting?

When I was in college, I concentrated on fiction—short stories and poetry—and did some freelance work. Although I find little time for writing other than my newspaper work, I still try to employ the same techniques I began to develop as a writer of fiction. The best pieces are those that really tell a story, instead of merely spewing out facts. Investigative stories should have all the tension of a good mystery. With human interest stories, the reader should come away with more than just a vague idea of what the subject is all about. In the same way I tried to develop characters in short stories, I now try to give a full picture of those I interview.

Will you describe the process you normally go through in writing a story?

Often, I will try to find the "rhythm" of a story. I approach my writing much the way I approach dance or music. I can't plan how my body will respond to a certain type of music anymore than I can predict what will happen when I sit in front of my computer. I find it helpful to read a few passages or the entire story aloud so I can hear how they sound. In a spoken voice, I know if a passage rings true or not. Of course, this is sometimes difficult to do in the newsroom without annoying co-workers, but it's the only process that I consistently use while writing.

Do you outline, organize your notes, and so forth?

For most interviews, I use a tape recorder, which allows me to make notes to myself about other things: what a person is wearing, something intriguing that may be happening around them, the way they respond to certain questions.

What are the three problems you face most frequently in writing? How do you solve them?

I'm constantly battling clichés. Sometimes, especially when I'm on deadline, I want to do something different, but those clichés are just sitting there, calling my name, begging me to take the easy way out. To avoid that, I constantly try to look at conventional things in different, unusual ways. Of course, there's the oldest nemesis, writer's block, but my natural aversion to overtime helps me get past that most of the time. The biggest problem, which really isn't a problem at all, is the perpetual challenge to improve. One of the best things about working here is the willingness of co-workers to bestow compliments. It's nice to know my work is appreciated, but I can't ever allow that knowledge to make me think that I've reached my high point as a writer. As a constant reminder, I keep a small sticker with the title of a Public Enemy song affixed to my desk: "Don't Believe the Hype."

Will you say something about voice? Do you have a clear and individual voice you can tune to a particular story? How do you hear and tune your voice?

As I mentioned before, I read my stories aloud to hear their rhythm. As a writer, I adapt myself to the story's mood, using my "voice" to tell that story best. When I began to read John Cheever's short stories in high school, I found myself trying to write with his dry wit and flair for irony. It didn't work. Cheever's voice isn't my voice, whatever that may be. It's difficult to describe it, but I just know what sounds right for me as a writer.

What is your process of revision and editing? Do you have your own private checklist? If so, what is it?

I prefer to edit my stories on a printout. After staring at a computer screen for several hours, everything starts to blur together and it's more likely that I'll overlook mistakes or changes that need to be made. First, I check names, addresses, titles of organizations, etcetera. Then I recheck each quote and attribution to make sure I've got the right people saying the right things.

What advice do you have for beginning writers?

Be creative. Don't be afraid to try something your journalism professors distinctly told you to avoid. Be experimental, say a prayer, and send it to your editor. The worst they can do is send it back.

What books, authors, or publications have you found helpful as a writer that you would recommend to other people?

I've always been an admirer of Zora Neale Hurston, John Cheever, Toni Morrison and, recently, Armistead Maupin. Although each has a very distinct style, they all have an impeccable command of character development, dialogue, and setting. I've also learned a great deal about story development from film makers and screenwriters such as Billy Wilder and Paddy Chayefsky. And I'm still a big fan of Dr. Theodor Geisel, better known as "Dr. Seuss." The man practically invented literary minimalism.

What can a writer do to develop an effective relationship with an editor?

You have to cultivate editors to your writing style, leaving room for thoughtful criticism. An acrimonious relationship with an editor benefits no one, especially the writer. Don't be afraid to fight for your work— after all, your name is the only one that appears on the story—but remember nothing you write is carved in stone. At this stage in my career, I'm still developing my style and voice as a writer and welcome the advice of those interested in helping me hone my craft.

Develop:
Work on What Works

Many news stories are first-draft stories; that is the discipline we all share. We can deliver on deadline, usually by resorting to the stereotypes and clichés of journalism. But if newspapers are going to provide the reader with stories that are not broadcast in radio news flashes or caught in a few moments on the television evening news, we need to develop our first-draft stories.

The experienced writer learns to ignore, for the moment, the weak spots in a draft and attend to the strong areas. They are what need development. The strong parts of a draft—what works—may involve content or form or both. The writer pushes the material at this stage of the writing process.

In a second writing the writer may set up the quote, put a statistic in context, write in a more involved (or more detached) voice, develop a scene, emphasize a process, or reveal new dimensions to a personality.

The development of a draft may take moments or hours or

days, even weeks: The time a writer needs will expand to the time an editor allows. But it does not need to be a longtime project. It can be done between the reporting and writing of other stories, in fragments of time. And if the first draft is written at high velocity, then there is writing time left over to develop the draft.

The reader hungers for more revealing details, more information of all kinds, a clear sense of context, and a stronger and more personal voice. There should be enjoyment and satisfaction in developing a draft with pace and proportion, context, and significant information, all developed to the full potential of the material and the space available.

TWENTY FIVE

LAYERING

I'm doing so many writing projects that I can't concentrate on one each day, so I'm getting a novel done by writing 300 words (a page) a day. And it's working, but not in the way I expected.

I thought that I would write the pages sequentially, hup-two-three-four fashion . . . and I did in the beginning. But soon I found myself going back to the beginning of each chapter many mornings and working through the text, adding, cutting, developing, shaping. Since my software can count words, I count the words before I start to write, and quit after approximately 300 new words.

Counting words appears silly, but Ernest Hemingway, William Faulkner, Graham Greene, and many others found it a necessary discipline and so do I. If you want to get that book done, try it. Anal compulsives of the world, arise!

I've called the process of going over and over the text "layering," because it seems similar to what I've done when oil painting, adding layer upon layer until I achieve the texture that captures the subject. It's been fascinating to see what happens. Some days I let the dialogue run; other days I seem to work on characterization or description; at other times I'm developing the conflict between characters.

Layering is a helpful technique for newswriters who have the time to work on the long piece in which tone and texture are important. Many news stories are written over a series of days, and writing through the piece each day for several days helps develop and deepen a draft.

And it could also help you, as it has me, deal with the destructive pressure to produce perfect copy every day. As David Mamet reminds us: "As a writer, I've tried to train myself to go one *achievable* step at a time: To say, for example, '*Today* I don't have to be particularly inventive, all I have to be is *careful*,' and make up an outline of the actual physical things the character does in act one. And then, the following day to say, 'Today I don't have to be careful. I already have this careful, literal outline, and all I have to do is be a little inventive,' etcetera, etcetera."

The act of layering can be forgiving. We don't have to get it all right today, we just have to do a decent job on one element in the text.

We should always remember that there is no one way to write anything. I've published more than twenty books and each one seems to have been written differently. We have a tendency to limit ourselves in a harmful way when we approach each project as if all the writing tasks are the same. Eudora Welty reminds us, "The writer himself studies intensely how to do it while he is in the thick of doing it; then when the particular novel or story is done, he is likely to forget how; he does well to. Each work is new. Mercifully, the question of *how* abides less in the abstract, and less in the past, than in the specific, in the work at hand."

TWENTY SIX

NOTES ON NARRATIVE

We talk a lot about stories in newspapers, but we do not seem to understand the importance of story—that is, narrative—and to appreciate it and find ways to adapt it for the newspaper.

Story is the mother of all forms of writing. Despite some intellectuals' lack of respect for traditional narrative, it is the principal way we all, intellectuals included, explore, understand, and explain our world to each other. We live and believe by the narratives we have woven from our past and our experience. More than we realize, we see the world through story.

As one who has published novels and is working daily on one, I thought it might be interesting to make some notes on the craft of writing narrative so that you might see ways to make use of these skills in your stories.

Character

- Story best begins not with theme or plot but character.

- We read because we become involved with characters; we remember stories because of characters.

- As writers we need to develop characters that are believable as well as physically and psychologically complex; characters that writer and readers feel strongly about, in a compassionate way.

- We report what characters do and how they do it so that the characters reveal themselves to us and to our readers.

- We need to see the characters physically, *in action*.

Dramatic Action

- The evolving, natural interaction between the characters and their world makes the story move forward. Plot or ideas do not manipulate character, but characters reacting to each other reveal ideas and create the plot, or chain of action and reaction.

- The action and reaction must be significant to the characters. Significance or importance may be measured by the fact that the actor and reactor are changed by the action, which can rarely be reversed.

- Conflict is central to story. The characters' actions have an affect on one another: action and reaction.

- The action and reaction of the characters moves the story toward an actual or *implied* resolution.

- The writer does not tell the reader how to feel, what to think. The writer gets out of the way and gives the reader the experience of the story, and that causes the reader to think and feel.

External Dialogue

- Dialogue is action. "Get thee to a nunnery" is not just chatter, not to the woman involved. Dialogue is what characters do to one another.

- Characters speak to each other in a shared world. They do not give background they both know. They speak from a ground of common knowledge.

- Dialogue has the illusion of oral language. It should be written out loud, with your ear. It may consist of fragments, incomplete statements, or interruptions. Characters do not always listen to each other and respond directly to what is said.

- The dialogue must express its own emotion and its own meaning. Not "he said listlessly" or ". . . angrily"; not "he said stupidly" or " . . . intelligently."

- The simple "he said" and "she said" are unread but necessary *some* of the time. Most times it should be obvious who is speaking. The he-saids and she-saids pace the dialogue, provide a beat, and reinforce the meaning.

- The characters should sound different from the writer or narrator and from each other.

Internal Dialogue:

- The characters' thoughts are revealed through internal dialogue; the characters' talk within themselves, and their speech is not punctuated by quotation marks.
- The characters' thoughts are limited to each character's background and experience within the story and all the other restrictions of dialogue. The character does not reflect the knowledge and thinking of the author.
- The voice of internal dialogue must be appropriate to the character and the character's world.

Place

- The story takes place in a world. The reader should discover and experience that world as it is important to the actions of the characters.
- Description does not usually stand by itself, despite the teacher's instruction to write a descriptive paragraph. It is woven in.
- Description should be built of specific, *revealing* details, details that support the action and meaning of the story.
- Description should not move from left to right or top to bottom but convey a dominant impression from a focal point significant to the story.
- A character's action is a very efficient form of description. He sits down and the chair breaks; the reader discovers the character is as portly as a writing coach.

Person

- Stories are usually best told in the third person. The reader identifies most easily with third-person characters and they are most easily revealed in action.
- First person seems easy, but it is hard. How do you reveal the narrator's appearance, for example. The focus is limited to what the narrator can see, hear, know, or do.
- The second person (you) simply doesn't work.

Point of View

- Where the camera is placed. The reader can only see what the camera can see.

- The camera zooms back and in close. The closer in, the less the camera can see but the intensity increases; the further back, the larger the context and the greater the detachment.
- The usual places:
  –In the sky or the ceiling in one corner of the room.
  –In a character's forehead or in characters' foreheads.
  –Moving between both places—but not too often or too quickly.
- The reader stands beside the camera and can only see, hear, and know what the camera reveals.

Narrative Voice

- The voice or music of the story is as important as character and dramatic action. It reveals and supports the meaning of the story. It is the soundtrack and more.
- Reading is an individual act. The reader hears the story and likes to hear an individual voice speaking to an individual reader.
- The narrative voice is the natural voice of the writer tuned to the story. It is the way that this particular story must be told.
- The voice must be appropriate to the time, place, and nature of the story.
- A voice that delights the reader is consistent but has a series of small, appropriate, revealing surprises.

Exposition

- The trick is to use as little exposition as possible. Exposition is that material unimportant to the characters that must be told to the reader so that the reader will understand the story.
- Exposition, if necessary, is buried in the action of the story, including the actions or internal and external dialogue.

Scene

- Scene is the basic unit of narrative. It is the place where characters meet and interact in a setting.
- Stories, novels, plays, and movies move forward through a series of scenes in which an action takes place and its effect is felt, which causes a new action or scene.

Chronology

- Time in a story does not move forward equally. I find it helpful to think of a necklace with various-size beads on it. Time moves quickly between scenes that are developed in details. Years may be a blank space between scenes; a moment may take pages to develop and be revealed.
- The reader needs a sense of time moving forward, a clock ticking.
- A good rule is to have a story start as near the end as possible.
- A story should not have an introduction; the reader should be placed immediately in the story. The information the reader needs to understand the story should come as the reader needs it.
- A story should not end with a conclusion that tells the reader what it means. It's too late for that. The story should end with an action that causes the reader to come to his or her own conclusion.
- A flashback in time may be necessary but it is a failure of your chronology. Background information should be woven into the story and given to the reader as the reader needs it.

Theme

- Theme is the narrative in its entirety. To paraphrase Archibald MacLeish, a story should not mean, but be. The story is the statement of the theme or meaning of the story.
- The theme is usually discovered by the writer through the writing. The writer usually feels no need to articulate or reduce the story to a meaning.
- Each reader will find a different theme or meaning in the story depending on the background, the knowledge, the experience, and the psychological need of the individual reader.

These notes reflect the attitudes of one writer who is working on fiction. More news stories could be told as narratives, but it will be up to individual newswriters working on specific stories to teach us how that can best be done.

TWENTY SEVEN

ANALYSIS OF A RICHARD KNOX STORY

It seems appropriate to perform an autopsy on the work of a medical writer. I think we can learn by taking apart stories we admire or stories we have written (whether we have admired them or not) to see what works and how.

Richard Knox's "How luck, high-tech foiled 'sudden death'," starting on page one of the January 16, 1989, *Globe,* is worthy of careful examination. The topic is highly technical and so, to make the reader read and to dramatize the story, he decided to tell it through a narrative case history. Knox had to tune the story so that it was dramatic but not melodramatic, technical but not too technical:

Francis Jefferson, known as "Rindge" by his wide circle of friends, was having the time of his life on the evening of Dec. 5. Just retired from a satisfying 30-year career dealing with juvenile delinquents, Jefferson was master of ceremonies at a reunion of people who grew up in the Humbolt Avenue area of Roxbury in the early 1940s.

Knox takes two paragraphs to introduce you to the victim of the heart attack, convince you he is worth your concern, and set the scene for the always-unexpected "sudden death" attack.

It was a great occasion, drawing 600 people to the Prince Masonic Hall in the Grove Hall section of Dorchester. The program went off without a hitch. The music began. Jefferson started to dance with an old friend.

Today he remembers none of it. At 9:45 that evening, Jefferson's scarred, 62-year-old heart, over-stimulated by the excitement, suddenly fell into a wild, often-fatal dance of its own, known medically as ventricular fibrillation.

Now the pace changes. Notice how much more specific information Knox gives the reader. And the information is in context; it is delivered when the reader needs it. I was particularly impressed by the description of the beat as a dance (ironic since the victim was dancing) and the fact that the writer delivered the medical name after the definition.

It's sometimes called a "sudden death" heart attack, and it kills about 315,000 Americans each year—one every 100 seconds.

Now the incident is put in a larger, more meaningful perspective. And there is the message: This could be you.

Jefferson didn't die, and he almost certainly won't die the next time his heart goes haywire.

Knox is in a conversation with the reader, which is just the right place to be. The reader finishes this paragraph and asks, "Why?" Knox will now tell the reader.

The reasons why combine equal measure of luck and high-technology medicine. Jefferson's story tells a good deal about sudden cardiac death in Boston, and why the great majority who suffer cardiac arrest don't survive.

Here is an interesting organization device, important in all sorts of complex political, environmental, business, and budget stories. Knox lays out the topics he will deal with in the order he will deal with them.

First, the luck. Among the crowd was a nurse, Gloria Browne, who recognized what was going on and knew how to do cardiopulmonary resuscitation, as only a tiny fraction of citizens in this region do. Meanwhile, someone fetched help for the Engine 24–Ladder 23 station of the Boston Fire Department next door. Someone else called 911 at 9:45 p.m. The ambulance arrived 9 minutes later, an unusually fast response time for Boston, according to Boston emergency services officials.

The writer is very specific and specificity brings with it authority. Knox weaves in the fact that few local people know CPR, a theme that will emerge later in the article.

Knox is also fair in pointing out that the ambulance response time that may seem slow to the reader is unusually fast "for Boston," another topic to be dealt with later. He is weaving a number of threads through this story.

Next the technology came into play. Since last September, Boston's municipal ambulances have been equipped with portable defibrillators, programmed to recognize ventricular fibrillation and to shock a quivering heart back into normal rhythm.

Now he moves on to the next topic. Note the grace with which he works in definitions and the energy of such words as "quivering."

That's just what emergency medical technicians Paul Hughes and James Rattigan did. A few minutes behind them came the advanced life-support team of John Doyle and Brendan Kearney, paramedics trained to start intravenous lines, administer heart-quieting drugs and stabilize cardiac arrest victims en route to the hospital.

Neat, effective narrative that easily carries information to the reader.

By the time Jefferson arrived at Boston City Hospital, at 10:24 p.m., his pulse was normal and he was breathing on his own.

Jefferson is one of 104 cardiac arrests in Boston since the portable defibrillator came into use on September 20. Of those, only 33 were reached in time to try shocking the heart back to normal rhythm. The attempt was successful in 12 patients, but six died anyway before they got to the hospital.

Of the remaining six, only Jefferson has survived to be discharged from the hospital.

Again, Knox puts the story in perspective, albeit a pretty discouraging perspective. This reader wondered why the story was written if the figures were so bad, then remembered that Jefferson was a special case. Okay, Knox, tell me how special and why I should know it.

But that's not the end of the tale. The most dramatic application of technology—the one that makes Jefferson's rescue more than just a temporary victory—was yet to come.

Now a transition paragraph and a promise to the reader.

On Christmas Day, Jefferson had another close brush with death. His 81-year-old mother, his sister and his brother-in-law had just arrived at Boston City Hospital to visit when he suddenly felt dizzy and blacked out. Doctors and nurses shooed the horrified family away as they once again shocked Jefferson back to life.

Another dramatic scene, and readers like scenes. This one reinforces the importance of what is going to happen to Jefferson.

Clearly, the drugs he was taking to block another episode of ventricular fibrillation were not working. Jefferson, who had survived a serious heart attack and two separate open-heart operations in the 1970s to bypass clogged coronary arteries, would almost certainly suffer anoth-

The writer gives me the case history when I need it. A more inexperienced writer might have tried to jam it into the lead.

er cardiac arrest after he left the hospital. And next time he might not be so lucky.

Without effective medication, about one-third of all sudden death survivors will have another episode within a year, studies have shown. Within two years half are dead.

More on how serious a condition Jefferson and others with his condition find themselves in.

Cardiologist Rodney H. Falk proposed another alternative, one that Jefferson had never heard of: implanting a miniaturized automatic defibrillator in his abdomen with wires leading to the heart. The next time ventricular fibrillation struck, the $15,000 machine would recognize the change in rhythm within six seconds, draw an electric charge from its batteries within another six seconds, and deliver a jolt of electricity powerful enough to quell the abnormal rhythm.

Now to the center of the story, just when we are impatient for it—and understand its significance.

Knox does an expert job of making technical detail clear to the average reader.

The shock is only about one-tenth as powerful as that delivered externally by a conventional defibrillator.

But it's enough to make its owners feel as though they've been kicked in the chest.

"It's as though you had an ambulance squad sitting in your chest," Falk told Jefferson. "You will do extremely well. Three years ago I couldn't tell you that. This device has revolutionized the care of patients in your situation."

The writer anticipates and answers the reader's question: What's it feel like?

"I was convinced this would make sense," Jefferson said Friday as he was preparing to go home from the hospital. "Partly because of the confidence Dr. Falk had in it. I had confidence in him."

I like hearing from the patient and seeing the decision from his perspective.

Surgeons implanted the automatic device in Jefferson 11 days ago in a lengthy operation during which they deliberately provoked his heart into fibrillation to test the system. Falk tested it again last Thursday, pushing Jefferson's heart over the brink, then watching tensely as the defibrillator jolted him back to life.

We are taken into the operating room to see and feel the tension in such an experimental technique. And this happens after we are concerned about the patient and understand the seriousness of his condition.

"He went out like a light," the cardiologist said. "Then suddenly he was awake again." Jefferson retains no memory of the life-saving shocks.

Later Friday, as he relaxed in his three-decker, Jefferson said his main emotion was gratitude for "All the people who did something to save me. The system saved me. The system worked."

Unfortunately, the system that worked for Jefferson fails for most "sudden death" victims.

A nice turn here that allows Knox to go beyond his case history to the larger issues in the story.

As Boston City Hospital doctors and emergency services personnel pointed out last week, implantable fibrillators are no good if people don't survive long enough to get to the hospital, or if they die at the hospital because their brains were

Knox is responsible. He doesn't just write a melodramatic, everything-is-wonderful story. He always keeps the story in an appropriate context.

devastated by lack of oxygen due to inadequate and sluggish care on the way there. And portable fibrillators on every ambulance are not enough if ambulances are too few, response times too slow and if too few ordinary citizens are trained to resuscitate cardiac arrest victims while waiting for emergency personnel to arrive.

"Mr. Jefferson had a lot of things going for him, but not everybody has," said David M. Ladd, director of training and special operations for Boston Emergency Medical Services. "The point needs to be made. We have the technology and the ability to save a lot of lives. The problem is we don't have enough of it. And somebody has to train the public."

Falk agreed. "The crucial message is to get medical care to cardiac arrest victims, not cardiac arrest victims to medical care," the cardiologist said.

"Citizens can do a far greater job than physicians can in reducing the toll of sudden death. We can only deal with the survivors, but the public can ensure there are more survivors for us to work on."

Richard Knox gets out of the way and lets authorities make his point for him.

The story was accompanied by a sidebar going into greater technical detail for those readers who were interested. The craft in this story is appropriate to the increasing number of complex stories that must be reported in a responsible newspaper. We can all learn from it.

TWENTY EIGHT

CASE HISTORY OF A COLUMN

My weekly "Over 60" columns usually begin with the ordinary. My eye catches a glint from an insignificant element in my life or the lives of those around me, and I see it suddenly with humor, anger, sadness, amusement, nostalgia, or concern. Emotion gives it significance.

Right here my writing of the case history was justified: I had never before fully understood the role emotion plays in making me see a story where I had not seen a story before. I wrote the last sentence and found it true when I read it. It reminds me to pay attention to how emotion focuses my attention. I may see more stories I have overlooked.

When I got home on Wednesday night recently I discovered I had left my daybook and date book at the *Globe*. Total panic. I didn't know what I had to do the next day, who to see, what to write. I called Tom Mulvoy and he understood! They were found and sent overnight. I noticed how dependent I, and my wife, had become on our notes to ourselves, our lists, our calendars.

I recommend having a special notebook or file cards or using your reporter's notebook to write down fragments that may become the germ of future stories. Writing them helps you remember them and often a special twist is added in the transcription.

As should happen to all of us on all stories, the material around us begins to organize itself into a pattern. I made a note in my daybook Thursday morning: "you can tell the old ones—we leave a trail of notes." That's enough to hold the idea in place. I might write about it this week or next August.

The next morning my eye caught that line, and I took about five or six minutes to draft the following on the word processor:

You can always find those of us who are Over Sixty. We leave a trail of paper.

We make notes in planners, on calendars, on 3 by 5 cards, in memo books, on the backs of envelopes, on the edges of paper torn from newspapers and magazines, on the backs of other notes, on re-recycled paper, on small colored pads of paper and on large white pads of paper.

We stick yellow notes, small medium and large, to the door where we will see them when we go out; to the door where we will see them on the way in. We put them on telephones, the refrigerator we still call the ice-box, on books, on the TV screen, on kitchen cabinets, on headboard and bureau, on chairs, cabinet doors, chair backs, on the auto dashboard.

[My wife added, in piles on the floor.]

But we never find the right note . . .

The three dots are a signal to myself that I may develop this or drop it or leave it.

And if we find an interesting one, it blurs. I wear tri-focals (which should be called try focals).

Try-focals was a typo. I liked it. Some of my best writing comes from typos. I wonder if I would write as well as I do if I couldn't type.

My neck clicks as I try one focal, then another and another, finally take them off and focus by placing the tip of my nose at the edge of the note.

Fifteen minutes later when I walk into the coffee table I try to find where I have put my glasses but that is another column.

When I do get the notes in range, I face problems in translation. Here are some recent examples from our home:

"Jfpx called. Pls call back at 779–8py8."

I always try to stop a draft at a point where I have a pretty good idea of what I'm going to do next if I am interrupted. That makes it easier to get back into the text.

[278 - 25 = 253 of 800]

The strange note at the end indicates I'm trying to satisfy my editor's request for 800 words, no more.

This came easily. It was ripe. If it hadn't come easily, I would have dumped it. If the idea has validity, it will come again. If I had to write on assignment and the lead didn't come easily, I would draft a dozen, fifteen, two-dozen leads as fast as possible, about three minutes each, until I got one I could go with. The time spent on leads speeds up the rest of the writing for me. What I was looking for was a voice for this text. I think I found it—and my first reader, my wife, agrees—but I will not know until I write it and my editor reads and responds.

Here is my first draft, warts and all:

You can always find those of us who are Over Sixty. We leave a trail of paper.

We make notes in planners; on calendars; on 3 by 5 cards; in memo books; on the backs of envelopes, sales slips, doctors' appointment cards; on the edges of paper torn from newspapers and magazines; on the backs of other notes; on re-recycled paper; on small colored pads of paper; on long, yellow legal pads; on the telephone message, stationery, pads of paper we were "given" by our employer in the years before we retired.

We stick yellow notes, small medium and large, to the door where we will see them when we go out; to the door where we will see them on the way in. We put them on telephones, use magnets to attach them to the refrigerator we still call the ice-box, on books, on the TV screen, on kitchen cabinets, on headboard and bureau, on chairs, cabinet doors, chair backs, on the auto dashboard, in piles on the floor where we may see them as we step around the other stuff we've left on the floor so that we will see it.

But if we find a note that looks interesting, it blurs. I wear tri-focals [which should be called try focals]. My neck clicks as I try one focal, then another and another, finally taking them off and focus by placing the tip of my nose at the edge of the note.

Fifteen minutes later when I walk into the coffee table I realize I'm unglassed and try to remember where I have put my spectacles but that is another column.

When I do get the notes in range, I face problems in translation. Here are some recent examples from our home:

- *"Jfpx called. Pls call back 779-8py8."*
- *"Ripe shoes."*
- *"Car needs introspection. Lube loys torque."*
- *"Frg773x's birthday. Hurry anniversary. Gift?"*
- *"Bk. Monster cd. py due."*

- *"A peel tx asses 4 pm. Bring s5ttly fl."*
- *"Bnans. Oat mgrp. chp wne. rgyt juc."*
- *"Call frd abt slumba prty."*
- *"Put inbgyttr in mal. tdy."*
- *"Wagratater!!!!!"*

My wife starts laughing to herself in the car. That's less worrisome than when she laughs in her sleep and can't remember why. "Why are you laughing?"

"Do you remember the Palmer Method?"

"Hours upon hours of making circles on the ball of your forearm."

"Your what?"

"That's what I used to ask but every teacher in our school knew what it meant."

"Could you read what they wrote on the board?"

"Sometimes."

And we both laughed. But it isn't funny when you are Over Sixty and can't remember if you keep a cat.

At our age, forgetting why you are standing in the hardware store or who you promised to call on the phone or the name of your best friend, brings terror.

Is it the first sign of what is it, that terrible disease we used to call sen something. Oh yes, senility. What's the other one? Al something, Alzheimer's? That's it.

I hear my self laughing nervously. Talking to yourself is one thing. Laughing out loud in an empty room is . . . Well, black humor worked in combat, I'll try in the Golden Years. There is absolutely nothing funny about Alzheimer's, but if I don't laugh, I'll whimper.

Still I need more comfort and I think back when I was young and my mind drifted off in class, how the coach would find me staring through a window he couldn't see during practice (sometimes in a game), how many times mother had to remind me to take out the garbage, how my sergeants used their own gentle forms of persuasion to get my attention when I forgot I was involved in participatory patriotism.

But returning to who I was as a teen-ager when I walked around gap-mouthed trying to find out where to put my hands and how the world worked wasn't very comforting.

Then I was saved by a news story. A California professor, Lofti A. Zadeh, has developed a computer theory called fuzzy logic. He has been scorned in the U.S. but Japan is using his fuzzy logic computer program to run trains, and they have just established a Laboratory for International Fuzzy Engineering Research with 36 million dollars.

I've got it. Mature memory is a higher form of thinking made necessary by a brain filled to capacity with wisdom. The resulting fuzzy memory leads directly to fuzzy thinking and we'll find out what that means when I get the Center for Fuzzy Thinking funded. No one under sixty need apply.

[752 words]

Now I'll read it through, run the spell check, and have my wife read it. I made only a few changes, just a touch of fine tuning here and there for clarification and a bit more to make sure the reader doesn't think I think Alzheimer's is funny.

Here I did something unusual. I submitted the column in draft to several of the seminars of *Globe* writers and editors and received several suggestions. I wish I had the time to have a panel of writers and editors read everything I write. Books these days sometimes get so little editing; I have to exploit my friends to help me see my draft anew.

Here are what my readers said:

- Some thought the lead was especially good. One said it wasn't only Over Sixtys who leave trails of paper. True, but I'm writing the "Over Sixty" column and focussing on the impact at that age.

- Many liked the way I let the detail pile up. They thought I paced that well, that it needed such length to have an impact. Several liked ice-box and auto dashboard, terms no young writer would use. One said too much, too much. I had wondered if it was too much myself and I had thought of new things to add. I read it carefully and made changes.

- The list got a lot of attention. Everyone liked it but some were confused and I had to make sure they got the joke. Will cut slumba party. Takes reader off on an imaginary trip, as it suggests an orgy of old-timers in Doctor Denton's. My editor, who was part of the seminar, wanted four items, others wanted six, but most wanted fewer than my ten.

- Most of the *Globe* seminar members were too young to remember the Palmer Method. ALL people over sixty will remember, but I have young readers, too. Can I sneak in a definition? Is it worth saving or should I cut it all?

- We had an interesting discussion at the point when I said that we oldies fear forgetting because it seems a symptom of Alzheimer's. Some thought I should set up the terror of memory loss when you are over sixty more dramatically. I thought that was a given in my audience and I could play on terror they have. No need to dramatize it. I promise to read it through carefully to decide who's right.

- One writer thought I could cut the last line of the paragraph beginning "Is it the first sign . . ." and the last sentence of the column. I agreed.

- I worried that I might offend somebody who has Alzheimer's in their family. No one thought I would. It was very important for me to hear that. Many times someone else will catch a tone or a hidden insensitivity of which I am not aware.

- A couple of readers thought I could cut the teen-age stuff. Another writer pointed out that the sentence beginning "But returning . . ." made the reader take a long trip between subject and verb. I agreed instantly, knowing if I kept it, I'd clean it up. One editor strongly urged me to include a note on the research that explains why we lose memory as we age. I considered both suggestions seriously, knowing I could not make the decision on the teen-ager stuff until I had done the research on the other issue. If I include that research, it may affect the tone, length, proportion, and pace of the column.

I edited the column, accepting, adapting, or disregarding their comments. Disregarding after careful consideration. If one person misreads what I've read, I don't get defensive. If one person misses the point, others may.

I thought I was done with the column and moved it into the appropriate directory. Here's the column after my editing.

You can always find those of us who are Over Sixty. We leave a trail of paper.

We make notes in planners; on calendars; on 3 by 5 cards; in memo books; on the backs of envelopes, sales slips, doctors' appointment cards; on the edges of paper torn from newspapers and magazines; on the backs of other notes; on re-recycled paper; on small colored pads of paper; on long, yellow legal pads; on the office stationery we "borrowed" before retiring.

We stick yellow notes, small medium and large, to the door where we will see them when we go out; to the door where we will see them on the way in. We put them on telephones, use magnets to attach them to the refrigerator we still call the ice-box, on bookmarks, on the TV screen, on kitchen cabinets, on headboard and bureau, on chairs, cabinet doors, chair backs, on the auto dashboard, in piles on the floor where we may see them as we step around the other stuff we've left on the floor so that we will see it.

But if we find a note that looks interesting, it blurs. I wear tri-focals (which should be called try focals). My neck clicks as I try one focal, then another and another, finally take them off and focus by placing the tip of my nose at the edge of the note.

Fifteen minutes later when I walk into the coffee table I realize I'm unglassed and try to remember where I have put my spectacles but that is another column.

When I do get the notes in range, I face problems in translation. Here are some recent examples from our home:
- *"Jfpx called. Pls call back at 779-8py8."*
- *"Ripe shoes."*
- *"Car needs introspection. Lube loys torque."*
- *"Mail cat. Rtrn old stmach. Nude dinr tnite."*

My wife starts laughing to herself in the car. That's less worrisome than when she laughs in her sleep and can't remember why. "Why are you laughing?"

"Do you remember the Palmer Method of penmanship?"

"Hours upon hours of making circles on the ball of your forearm."

"Your what?"

"That's what I used to ask but every teacher in our school knew that it meant your forearm muscle."

"Could you read what they wrote on the board?"

"Sometimes."

And we both laughed. But it isn't funny when you are over sixty and can't remember if you keep a cat.

At our age, forgetting why you are standing in the hardware store or who you promised to call on the phone or the name of your best friend, brings terror.

Is it the first sign of what is it, that terrible disease we used to call sen something. Oh yes, senility. What's the other one. Al something?

I hear myself laughing nervously. Talking to yourself is one thing. Laughing out loud in an empty room is . . . Well, black humor worked in combat, I'll try it in the Golden Years. There is absolutely nothing funny about Alzheimer's, but if I don't laugh, I'll whimper.

Still I need more comfort and I think back when I was young and my mind drifted off in class, how the coach would find me staring through a window he couldn't see during practice (sometimes in a game), how many times mother had to remind me to take out the garbage, how my sergeants used their own gentle forms of persuasion to get my attention when I forgot I was involved in participatory patriotism.

But returning to who I was as a teen-ager when I walked around gap-mouthed trying to find out where to put my hands and how the world worked wasn't very comforting.

Authorities say that memory loss is normal and that it shouldn't cause panic. When you relax the names will come to you. They may be right. I remember them at 3 the next morning when I no longer remember what I wanted to do with the name.

B. F. Skinner, now 85, says that we oldies forget names "because names have so little going for them by way of context."

I have a different theory. A California professor, Lofti A. Zadeh, has developed a computer theory called fuzzy logic. He has been scorned in the U.S. but Japan is using his fuzzy logic computer program to run trains, and they have just established a Laboratory for International Fuzzy Engineering Research with 36 million dollars.

I've got it. Mature memory is a higher form of thinking made necessary by a brain filled to capacity with wisdom. The resulting fuzzy memory leads directly to fuzzy thinking and we'll find out what that means when I get the Center for Fuzzy Thinking funded. No one under sixty need apply.

Then I read it over. I started making little changes, a comma here, a dash; then I came to the word "translation" and in fixing that I began to play with the text.

A reading by a colleague or an editor will often make me return to the text and see new possibilities in it. My editor liked the column, but in "fixing" it, the text started in a new direction and I followed. I always follow the text when it moves under my hand. I may not go where it goes, but I have to follow to see where it wants to take me. More often than not, the text knows where I should go better than I do.

I was having fun and what I sent in was changed—for the better, I think. My editor was surprised but pleased. She said, "This proves good writing is rewriting." We made a few minor changes and this is how it was published April 11, 1989. The revision only took about half an hour, but it was fun to do and I think the result was a better column.

I can't remember when my own rewriting of an article, poem, or book (fiction or nonfiction) didn't make it better. (I need editors to question my drafts and make suggestions, but editors' revisions of what I thought was my final draft haven't always been successful in my opinion.) I don't do as much rewriting now as I did when I was freelancing magazine articles and went through each one thirty times. Much of my writing is first draft these days. After fifty years of rewriting, and being rewritten, I should be able to produce a good first draft once in awhile.

Memories are made of . . . paper

By Donald M. Murray
Special to the Globe

You can always find those of us who are Over 60. We leave a trail of paper.

We make notes in planners; on calendars; on 3-by-5 cards; in memo books; on the backs of envelopes, sales slips, doctors' appointment cards; on the edges of paper torn from newspapers and magazines; on the backs of other notes; on re-recycled paper; on small colored pads of paper; on long, yellow legal pads; on the office stationery we "borrowed" before retiring.

We stick yellow notes, small, medium and large, to the door where we will see them when we go out; to the door where we will see them on the way in. We put them on telephones, use magnets to attach them to the refrigerator we still call the icebox, on bookmarks, on the TV screen, on kitchen cabinets, on headboard and bureau, on chairs, cabinet doors, chair backs, on the auto dashboard, in piles on the floor where we may see them as we step around the other stuff we've left on the floor so that we will not forget it.

But if we find a note that looks interesting, it blurs. I wear trifocals (which should be called try focals). My neck clicks as I try one focal, then another and another, take my glasses off and focus by placing the tip of my nose at the edge of the note.

Fifteen minutes later when I walk into the coffee table I realize I'm unglassed and try to remember where I have put my spectacles—but that is another column.

When I do get the notes in range, I face problems in understanding what I—or my wife—wrote to remind us:

"Jfpx called. Pls call back at 779-8py8."

"Ripe shoes."

"Car needs introspection. Lube loys torque."

"Mail cat. Rtrn old stmach. Nude dinr tnite."

And we were both trained in the Palmer Method, in good old-fashioned schoolhouses where we practiced circles and ovals and up and downs by the hour.

We laugh—nervously, very nervously—but it isn't really funny when you are Over 60 and can't remember the name of your cat—or if you keep a cat.

At our age, forgetting why you are standing in the hardware store, or whom you promised to call on the phone, or the name of your daughter, brings terror.

Is it the first sign of what is it, that terrible disease we used to call sen something. Oh yes, senility. What's the other one? Al something?

Again, I hear myself laughing nervously. Well, black humor worked in combat, I'll try it in the Golden Years, knowing there is absolutely nothing funny about Alzheimer's, but if I don't laugh, I'll whimper.

Still I need comfort right now, and I think back when I was young and I had a fine forgettery. I could forget a chore in three seconds flat and in class my mind was usually out the window. The coach would even find me heading the wrong way out of the huddle, and my sergeants used their own gentle forms of persuasion to get my attention when I forgot I was involved in participatory patriotism.

But I walked around gap-mouthed, empty of thought, when I was a teen-ager, and the idea that I am returning to that state isn't comforting.

Authorities, usually young authorities who can remember their statistics, tell me that memory loss is normal and that it shouldn't cause panic. They promise that when I relax the names will come to me. They are right. I remember the names at 3 the next morning when I no longer remember why I wanted the name.

A California professor, Lofti A. Zadeh, has developed a computer theory called fuzzy logic. He has been scorned in the United States, but Japan has just established a Laboratory for International Fuzzy Engineering Research with $36 million and is using his fuzzy logic computer program to keep trains running on time.

That's it. Adult-onset fuzzy memory is a higher form of thinking caused by a brain filled to capacity with wisdom.

Brag about achieving fuzzy memory. Wear a fuzzy memory T-shirt, "I'm Old and Wise. I Don't Need to Know Your Name!" Make up a bumper sticker: "Have YOU Forgotten a Name Today?"

Forget with pride.

TWENTY NINE

Interview:
SUSAN TRAUSCH

Susan Trausch has the ability to be witty on deadline. She has worked just about every beat in journalism, distinguishing herself in the business section, as a member of the Washington Bureau, and now as an Op Ed–page columnist.

How do you get ideas for your columns?

Pray.

Actually, ideas come from just living and doing the daily battle— standing in line at the bank and always being in the wrong one; spending a day trying to get the funny noise out of the car and discovering it's a tube of lipstick under the seat; living in an apartment with cardboard walls; having your credit card rejected in front of your fellow man. I write about the little annoyances that are big pains, and those are everywhere.

How do you decide which ideas to use?

I carry a notebook at all times, except when I really need one, and put ideas and experiences in it. When there's a bunch collected on a subject— say, embarrassing moments, or funny things people do at farm stands—I might write it. Then again I might not. This is a very mystical process, deciding what to use and when, and I don't know how I do it. Sometimes a news story will kick off an idea. Sometimes an idea I haven't thought about for five years will resurface and seem relevant and writable. I like to pick something that has roots attached to it and says something about human nature or the way we live. The key is wanting to write it. The idea has to come easily or it's not the right one.

How do you recognize when an idea is working or not working?

Sometimes I do. Sometimes I don't. The best thing is to get away from it and come back fresh. I usually write a draft on Monday and then put it away until Thursday or Friday morning. There's nothing like the sinking feeling of picking up a dud on Thursday.

It's a dud when the rhythm is off or the central idea doesn't hold together or it's loaded with clichés. The hardest part of writing a humor column is hitting the right rhythm. If one word is off in a sentence it clunks, and so I have to keep listening for the beat, starting at the top and reading and rereading. When I jump into the middle or work on one paragraph too long, I lose the timing. A paragraph can hang together just fine by itself and have perfect grammar, but it can louse up the whole flow of the piece if it moves too slowly or too quickly.

Writing a column is very different from writing a story. A story I can work on into the wee hours or do quickly on deadline. But if someone said to me, "Give me a column by three o'clock," I couldn't do it. I wouldn't trust what came out. I need those days away from it.

What process do you go through in writing the column?

It helps if I have the lead and tone before I start, but even then it's never easy. By nighttime I'm more exhausted than on any other day of the week. It's a whole day of going inside yourself, playing with intangibles, roping in feelings, and trying to make it all dance on paper. I love doing it, but I sweat it.

Are you aware of your voice when you write?

I'm very much aware of voice and try to write the way I talk. But at the same time I'm trying to keep myself out of it. It's a constant battle of the "I's." The temptation is to keep starting sentences with "I," but the best writing talks about "you" and "us."

What do you do to find a good ending?

The ending is as important as the lead in a humor column. It has to be a line that echoes the theme of the piece and ties it together.

What's the worst problem you face and how do you try to solve it?

Getting stuck or not being able to start. I try to solve it by writing fragments, phrases, anything, just as long as something is going on the paper, or the screen as we say in VDT land. Eventually a fragment turns into a sentence that turns into a paragraph.

Besides writing the column you do business stories. Do you have any advice for beginning reporters who are assigned to write in a specialized field?

Ask dumb questions. Better to make a fool of yourself in front of the boys at the First National Bank than to do it for the world in print. You just look the man in the eye and say, "Tell me, what exactly is the GNP, anyway?"

You had a year off at Stanford to look at the press from a distance. What worries you?

I think we should fight the "boys-on-the-bus" syndrome and not immediately cover something just because the *Times* or the *Post* did it. We should remember not to get carried away with our own power. The phrase "media star" should be a contradiction in terms. We should be nonentities, Columbos in ratty raincoats, just asking a few questions, if you wouldn't mind, ma'am.

What is the best advice on writing you've received?

It comes from O. Henry: "Write what makes you happy."

THIRTY

Interview:
MARY SIT

I admire Mary Sit for her ability to do a range of complex stories in a manner that entices me into reading them and allows me to understand them. She was interviewed as a new member of the *Globe* staff and looks at her job from that perspective. At the present she reports on real estate news.

Sit is a native Texan who grew up in Houston, Japan, Hong Kong, Taiwan, and England. She was graduated from the University of Houston, majoring in Journalism, and had a fellowship at the Institute of Journalism Education, University of California, Berkeley.

She worked as a television producer/reporter at an ABC-affiliate in Austin, Texas and, before coming to the *Globe,* worked one year at *The Day,* New London, Connecticut. Sit came to the *Globe* through a one-year minority internship program in September 1987 and became a staff reporter a year later.

Will you tell us the reporting and writing attitudes and techniques you use to bring clarity to complexity?

I never did business reporting before I came to the *Globe.* My first week was like trying to report the news in a foreign language without knowing how to count to ten in that language.

My basic rule of thumb is: If I can't understand the concept, then I can't explain it to readers or write about it intelligently.

I ask my sources tons of questions, including "dumb" questions, and force them to explain things on a level I can understand. Since business news is new to me, that can be a pretty basic level.

I don't make any assumptions in reporting. I over-report to make sure I've covered all the bases.

What homework do you do as a business writer?

When I first interviewed for a job here, Lincoln Millstein asked me: "How much business writing have you done?"

I replied, "Not much."

He said, "Don't worry about it. Just read the *Wall Street Journal* every day." And then he pointed out exactly what columns and stories to read.

Every night I take home a stack of papers: the *Wall Street Journal, New York Times,* and *Herald.* Of course, I read the *Globe* every morning.

What note-taking methods have you developed that work especially well on complex stories?

I took Gregg shorthand in high school because I knew back then I wanted to be a reporter. It helps tremendously out in the field.

In the office on phone interviews, I open a new file for each source and type notes directly into the computer. Immediately after the interview, I organize the notes, moving some paragraphs around and adding subheads in all caps.

I always put every source's name, title, and phone number at the top of the page. Nothing's more frustrating than scrambling through scraps of paper and scribbles when you have to call back a source.

Will you describe the kind of questions that produce the most information?

I think sometimes a certain attitude, rather than a proscribed list of questions, can produce the most information. By that, I mean if you're naturally very curious and genuinely interested in what a person has to say, projecting an "I care, I really want to know" attitude, a person is more apt to open up and go beyond the thirty-second soundbite.

How do you check complicated and contradictory information?

Ask the same questions to three or four experts in the same field. Pretty soon a certain theme emerges or a common thread appears that clarifies the picture. As a former teacher advised: "Report the hell out of your stories!"

Will you tell us how you organize a complicated story?

I use yellow highlighter pens and Post-it™ notes. Since I'm not comfortable using split screens and electronic files to write from, I make a printout of every interview, staple the pages, and spread them out on my desk.

I separate the stacks with Post-it™ notes: pro sources, anti sources, the experts, etcetera.

Will you describe how you write the draft of a complex story?

Before I write, I thoroughly read everything I've reported. I'll scan the supplemental, secondary material—the stuff the public-relations people send, old clips. If I haven't gotten an idea out in the field for my lead, this thorough re-reading usually triggers an idea. Sometimes, I'll jot down topics in rough outline form just to make sure I don't forget to include them in the story.

In the back of my mind, I'm always asking myself: What's the simplest way to say this? Would Mom understand this? (Mom is a concert pianist who learned to speak English at age fourteen and is now a businesswoman who subscribes to the *Wall Street Journal*.)

What are your most difficult reporting problems? How do you solve them?

Knowing when to stop reporting is hard for me. Especially when I'm excited about a topic, I tend to jump from one aspect to another to another, it's all so fascinating. But then it's difficult to narrow the focus again.

Deadline pressure solves this one. I stop because I have to start writing.

What are your most difficult writing problems? How do you solve them?

Creating metaphors or images that work in business stories is tough. I try to read lots of other people's business stories to see what they do. It's sometimes hard to paint pictures of business concepts that are still fuzzy to me.

Do you have reporters or writers who have been models for you?

I've observed and absorbed from the reporters around me. I admire Charlie Stein for the way he can take the most complicated economic story and explain it in a very clear, readable style, with wit and humor, too. Desiree French works nonstop and has the fastest turnaround from assignment to final copy. Teresa Hanafin is never too busy or too pressured to answer questions, be a verbal thesaurus, or listen to me "talk out" my story so I can figure out what I'm doing. David Mehegan writes business stories that don't sound like business stories. Some of Bruce Butterfield's stories read like the beginning of a bestseller.

What had you learned before you came to the Globe that has been especially valuable here?

I worked at a small paper where we were expected to turn out two stories a day and three on Friday. So I learned to work fast and meet deadlines.

I also learned to be selective in picking my battles.

What did you have to learn at the Globe?

I learned that we tell stories at the *Globe*. Don't just throw a bunch of facts at the reader; tell it in a compelling, dramatic fashion.

Who taught it to you and how? Or did you teach yourself?

My editors taught me—Lincoln Millstein, Steve Bailey, and Mary Jane Wilkinson. I came to the *Globe* through a one-year internship program that requires editors to evaluate you monthly. Lincoln would spend about an hour with me. He pointed out reporters I should observe. He demonstrated reporting techniques by acting out scenes.

Lincoln said the most important thing to learn is to write with confidence. Experiment with your writing and take chances. Steve did a lot of daily editing and would show me how to shape business news into interesting tales. Mary Jane would patiently listen to all my questions and concerns about a story and help me focus on a theme and the way to approach that. She was generous with positive feedback, which, of course, motivated me even more.

My editors were smart; by throwing a lot of stories at me they boosted my self-confidence.

What was the most surprising difference between the Globe *and where you had worked previously?*

The resources and pockets were deeper here. I could dial 2940 and a librarian would research clips for me. There were more tools available here to support the reporter.

How does the Globe *treat a beginning staff member? What could the* Globe *do better?*

I felt like my editors treated me like any other staff member. They needed me in business. I got real stories, not just wire stuff to rewrite. I tried not to think of myself as "the minority intern" but as a regular part of the team who was going to be around after twelve months.

The *Globe* could do a better job of introducing new reporters to the staff. And although I got a lot of support, I think some of the new reporters don't get the support and direction they need to excel.

What advice do you have for a young, beginning writer at the Globe?

Don't be afraid to ask questions. Walk into your editor's office and get his or her attention. Ask your colleagues for help. Since you're a so-called "young beginner," most will not feel threatened by you and are glad to answer questions.

Find out what your editor values in a reporter, really listen to what he or she is telling you, then follow that advice. Do it their way first; later, once you know you've won their respect, trust your own instincts.

Clarify:
Represent the Reader

Now the effective writer turns on his or her own copy, working through it with the eyes of an enemy reader who has little interest in the subject, has a large dollop of skepticism, and is in a hurry to turn the page.

The writer must detach himself or herself from intent, not reading what is supposed to be on the page but what *is* on the page.

This is not punishment but a central satisfaction of craft. "What makes me happy is rewriting," says Ellen Goodman. "In the first draft you get your ideas and your theme clear, if you are using some kind of metaphor you get that established, and certainly you have to know where you're coming out. But the next time through it's like cleaning house, getting rid of all the junk, getting things in the right order, tightening things up. I like the process of making writing neat. Bernard Malamud adds, "I love the flowers of afterthought."

It is usually most efficient to read the draft three times: very fast to see if there is a single dominant meaning; at half-speed to see if the draft is ordered and developed and that each important point is supported by evidence; then slowly to hear and tune the language so that the text has accuracy, clarity, and grace.

Experienced writers read by ear as much as by eye, hearing the draft paragraph by paragraph, sentence by sentence, phrase by phrase, word by word. The best writers become their own first editors, reading the draft as it will most certainly be read by a reader—in haste and with skepticism. Newswriters have to make their copy lively, compelling, accurate, clear, and as short as possible, adding and taking away, reading and writing to be read.

THIRTY ONE

TUNING YOUR VOICE

Listen to writers talk about voice, the music that carries the text to the reader.

Raymond Carver:

I think that a writer's signature should be on his work, just like a composer's signature should be on his work. If you hear a few bars of Mozart, you don't need to hear too much to know who wrote that music, and I'd like to think that you could pick up a story by me and read a few sentences or a paragraph, without seeing the name, and know it was my story.

John Fowles:

The most difficult task for a writer is to get the right "voice" for his material; by voice I mean the overall impression one has of the creator behind what he creates.

Michael Harper:

You have to shape the word, sing in dimensions, and layer the harmonies and jurisdictions implicit in design. It's a great discovery, the voicing of meaning.

Eudora Welty:

Ever since I was first read to, then started reading to myself, there has never been a line read that I didn't *hear*. As my eyes followed the sentence, a voice was saying it silently to me. It isn't my mother's voice, or the voice of any person I can identify, certainly not my own. It is human, but inward, and it is inwardly that I listen to it. It is to me the voice of the story or the poem itself.

Voice is the most important element in newspaper writing. Reporting produces the accurate, specific, revealing material that is the raw material of good writing but it is voice that makes the reader understand and care.

Voice illuminates fact; voice makes confusing information clear; voice makes what appears insignificant significant; voice attracts and holds readers, compels readers to think and to feel.

Voice is an individual human voice tuned to the purpose of its message and the ear of the reader. The tuned voice is the voice of the text. That is what the writer listens to while drafting and revising.

Tuning the voice of the text is the most complex writing activity. We must deal with layer upon layer of concern:

- Is this the right word?
- Is this the right word for the words just before it and just after it?
- Is this the right group of words in a sentence?
- Is this the right sentence for the paragraph?
- Is this the right paragraph for the draft?

We learn to read, rewrite, reread, and rewrite simultaneously just before we start to put words on the page, while we draft or while we revise and edit, working in split seconds between the particular and the whole. And if we are to keep improving as writers we need, from time to time, to go back and consider what we are doing so that we can develop and improve our writing instinct.

The Elements of Voice

It is as difficult to capture voice as it is to box the perfume of spring, but I think there are four basic elements in an effective voice:

Angle of vision. Where the writer stands in relation to the subject.

Precision of language. The right word in relation to the words surrounding it.

Position of information through language to provide emphasis, pace, and flow.

Music of the text that carries and supports what is being said.

Tuning for Angle

Voice begins with the way the writer views the subject. The writer's biography, experience, knowledge of the subject, and attitude towards the subject all affect the writer's voice.

Vantage Point

The place where the writer stands will be the place from which the reader views the subject. That place is usually influenced by personal and professional concerns.

Personal. Each of us sees the world in our own way. When he was reporting from Panama, Diego Ribadeneira had a special understanding of the Latin American attitude toward the U.S. military operation. If I had been there, I would have had special understanding of the feelings of the soldiers in the Eighty-second Airborne, having been in combat with the Eighty-second. Each of us would use language a bit differently to take advantage of personal vantage points.

Professional. We also see the world as journalists, we know how to view events so that we can turn the stream of confusion into a coherent news story, on deadline. We always stand a bit apart, reporting what is going on with some degree of professional detachment, and our voice reflects that attitude.

Focus

Voice selects. The words we use and their setting in phrase, sentence, and paragraph limits the subject and forces the reader to concentrate on significant elements in the story. Voice is framed by our language.

Distance. The writer's voice establishes the distance that the writer, and therefore the reader, stands from the subject; the voice may bring the reader in close and move the reader back in a pattern calculated to reveal meaning.

Tuning for Precision

Mark Twain said, "The difference between the right word and the almost-right word is the difference between lightning and a lightning bug." We begin tuning the voice of the text by seeking the right word, the right phrase, the right sentence, the right paragraph.

Accuracy

The reader will not long listen to the writer if the reader does not trust, and trust is earned by the truth of the material the reader knows. If the reader finds the writer making errors of fact, then the reader will not trust anything the writer says. The word—and the evolving combinations of words—that make up the voice must be accurate. Red hair must be red. But truth is not a matter of checking each fact in isolation. When I was at *Time,* a checker put a dot over every word. The details were accurate but they were not always (some would say not often) accurate in context. The voice of the text must be tuned so that it can be trusted.

Specificity

A lively voice depends on specific, revealing details. In tuning my voice, I find that one of the elements I concentrate on the most is making the text increasingly specific.

Tuning for Position

Until I started writing this piece, I did not realize the importance of position in voice and the many factors that influence the position of information in the voice of the text.

Emphasis

It is voice that tells the reader what is important and there are some positions that emphasize information more than others. In a paragraph, for example, the point of the greatest emphasis is at the end, the next greatest in the beginning, the least in the middle. As we tune the voice of the text we move words that emphasize the meaning of the material to those points.

Sequence

The voice of the text moves the reader through the story in a logical manner so that the full meaning of the draft comes clear under the reader's eye.

Pace

Pace establishes the speed that the reader will move through the text, slowing down, for example, when a complex idea needs to be understood and speeding up during the chase. Voice adjusts the varying speed of the text so that it clarifies meaning.

Flow

Pace is closely allied to flow, the energy that moves the reader through the text in a pleasing and compelling manner.

Readers

Voice anticipates the reader's need for information, the reader's questions, and responds to them. The text is tuned to the reader's ear so that it will be heard in the way the writer desires.

Tuning for Music

Each piece of writing has music, it has melody, it has a beat, it has a sound that the reader hears. It is the challenge of the hearing writer to tune the music in the text's voice so that it clarifies and communicates the meaning of the text.

How You Can Encourage Voice

Voice is the most personal quality in writing; the writer's voice reveals the writer.

In Yourself

To hear your voice, you have to write with your own language, in your own way. That means you have to accept yourself and write in the way that is right for you. Your voice is composed of your ethnic heritage, your family and neighborhood experience, your education, and your professional training. You have to hear your own voice, your natural way of writing so that you know the raw material you have to develop.

Then you have to adapt, or tune, your voice to the text, developing a text voice that expresses the meaning of the draft within all the professional limitations of time, space, tradition, and audience.

In Others

We tend to try to make everyone the same, to concentrate on a beginning writer's failure to write in the language we expect. If we want to develop voice we have to look positively at difference, to see what is unusual and specific in the writer's individual way of writing. Then, by respecting that voice, we can teach the writer to respect his or her own voice, to hear it, and *then* to tune it to the traditions of the writing task. If we are lucky, the writer's individual voice will remain strong and we can encourage the writer to use it to extend those traditions.

THIRTY TWO

REWRITING AND EDITING YOUR OWN COPY

John Ciardi once said that writing is "a schizophrenic process. To begin passionately and to end critically; to begin hot and to end cold; and, more important, to try to be passion-hot and critic-cold at the same time."

And it doesn't get any easier. The more experience we have, the more we know, the stronger the critic becomes. Yet unless we ignore the censoring editor within us, we will not produce a draft worth editing.

I have an idea for a column, just sort of an idea, a hint, an idea of an idea, and the critic within me snorts, "So what?" I've learned to escape the critic or, at least, to give myself the illusion I've cut through an alley, taken the subway to an unexpected stop, and doubled back, hiding my idea under my coat. But the critic affects the idea. I have to cultivate my potential topic, find its central tension, and put the idea into language—maybe just fragments of language, but enough to get a feel for it, enough to allow me to start writing before the critic snuffs out the column that might become.

As I write I have to make the critic work with me, making use of my craft (my critical skills, the traditions of my trade, and my language) to unleash meaning. I feel I am running ahead of the critic but, of course, I am not. I am running in harness with all I know about writing, trying to be free within my professional experience, trying to use my craft to say what I have not yet said before in a way that is appropriate to the emerging message. I try not to be limited by my craft but to use it to extend what I can say and how I can say it.

And then the draft is done. Now I must be critical, stand back, and try to see it with a reader's eyes. I am my own editor and the balance shifts so that the editor within me takes over reading the whole, the part, the line, and then the word, challenging everything: the meaning, the music, the pacing, the language, the form, the authority. Each trick of my craft comes under scrutiny, especially those of which I am most proud.

But still I cannot be editor alone. When I first started writing, I was word drunk, happy with whatever appeared on my page. Rejection—nothing less—made me critical. I began to get published and I became too critical, too cautious; so the pendulum has swung back and forth between birth-pride and self-disgust. I destroyed articles, stories, poems, and books that I now realize could have, and should have, been published.

As I am editor to my final draft, I have to keep the writer at work, challenging the editor within me so that I save those surprises of meaning and technique that work. The writer is continually engaged in a civil war between freedom and discipline, a war that must never be won or lost but must always continue, providing the tension that is essential to our craft.

Before writing we have to be aware of what has been written previously and how it has been written, but we have to be open to the unexpected, ready to welcome surprise in content and in approach.

During writing we have to employ all the lessons of our craft but push against them, encouraging those accidents of insight and style that produce significant, lively writing.

After writing we have to understand what we have written and make sure others understand it. The critic within us takes over as we make sure that what we say is accurate in detail and context; that what we say is graceful and clear.

Rewriting and Editing Before Writing

I used to think I wrote and then I edited (or was edited), but I have come to realize that my editors, internal and external, are always with me from idea through final draft. And the editorial role changes as I move through the writing process. In the beginning the critic is important but has to be resisted, or at least kept under control; in the middle of producing the text, critic and creator have to work in harmony; at the end the critic takes over.

Where is the revealing tension in the story?

Each good story unwinds as a tension within it is released. The reader confronts a surprise, new information that affects a previously believed truth, a conflict, a question, an unexpected problem, a solution to an old problem, a contradiction, or a story behind a story and is compelled to read on. Before writing, the writer should find the central tension that will release *this* story.

Who should read the story and WHY?

To edit your story effectively, you have to know a reader who needs the information the story provides or will enjoy discovering that information. To know what will make the reader pursue the story, you have to understand *why* the reader needs or enjoys the information. Will the reader read from fear, because of curiosity, because the information is of practical value, because it is funny, because it makes the reader mad, sad, laugh, or identify with the victim, because it makes the reader think or escape or feel, or because it changes the reader's vision of the world? There are many reasons but the effective writer identifies one that will connect this paper's readers with this story.

What form do I think will communicate the meaning effectively?

Form is meaning. When we use narrative, we say that the information we need to communicate has a beginning, a middle, and an end, organized by time. A profile says that people control, or powerfully influence, events; an interview says that someone has something important to say. We must make sure that the form we choose supports the meaning we have to communicate.

What do I think will be the effective voice of the story?

Voice is the magic in writing: an individual human voice is recorded in silent symbols on the page and then, or hours or years later, is heard in the reader's ears. It is that individual quality of voice that attracts and holds readers, communicates an attitude toward the story, and makes the meaning of the story clear and believed. The trick is to tune your voice so that it calls attention not to the writer but to the meaning of the story.

What length and shape do I expect the story to develop?

When I first taught I resented the students' question, How long do you want my paper to be? I thought it an indication of laziness or excessive concern with grades. But it is a profound question. The size of the canvas affects the picture. Give me a Sistine ceiling and I will do something different than on a Grumbacher 8-by-10 canvas. The entire conceiving of the story, the reporting as well as the writing, depends on a concept of length and shape. Of course, stories will change (grow or shrink) during the reporting or the writing, and then the writer has to consult with the editor to adjust their shared vision of how the story will appear.

Rewriting and Editing During Writing

It is important to write as dumbly as possible, a talent with which I was born and which I have developed through the years, despite teachers and editors. The writer has to give himself or herself over to the story, writing with natural instinct and with the instinct of craft (those skills which have been absorbed into our "natural" writing process). Yet the head intrudes. We stand back from the canvas during the making process, and during those moments we may consider some of the following questions—or hold them until the draft is done.

What's the promise of the lead?

It must be answered. Each lead is a contract with the reader. Significance or help or enjoyment or understanding or something else is offered to the reader who stays with the story. We must make sure we can deliver on our promise or we must go back and write a lead with a promise we can deliver.

Does the voice of the story support its meaning?

Clever writing or dull writing draws the reader away from the meaning of the story. We must tune our language to the voice appropriate to this story and to our readers. We must never forget that the music of the story is communicating meaning as much as information, organization, documentation, or form—perhaps more.

How does this paragraph move the story forward?

When I first started doing magazine pieces a writer, the late Hannah Lees, gave me a gift. She told me to write one paragraph to a page and for years I cut paper into half sheets and followed her counsel. I had been writing all over the place, spreading under- and over-developed paragraphs through my drafts (I averaged about thirty per magazine piece).

When I wrote a paragraph to a page, I began to learn the importance of the paragraph and how to develop one idea in a paragraph so that it moved the reader's understanding of the story forward.

Does the pace keep moving the reader forward but allow the reader time to absorb each point?

Timing is rarely talked about in writing, but the writer, like the comic, has to pace the delivery so that the reader is not allowed to escape but is allowed time to absorb each point before moving on to the next one. Reading aloud helps the writer to hear and judge the pace.

What would make the reader believe what I'm saying?

Most of us grow lazy in documenting our pieces. We grab whatever is handy or what we're comfortable with using, sprinkling our stories with quotes or statistics, anecdotes or references, instead of choosing the appropriate form of evidence to support the point being made.

What would make the reader care about what I'm saying?

Should we appeal to emotions? Yes, if it is appropriate. It is important that we make our readers feel as well as think. They need to meet the people in the story, see the effect of the event on those people, and observe the impact of the story. We should not tell the reader *how* to feel with summary words (sad, beautiful, tragic, happy) but give the reader an experience that will make the reader feel. As Mark Twain said, "Don't say the old lady screamed—bring her on and let her scream."

Does each point answer a reader's question and ask a new one?

Remember that each story is a conversation with the reader. The reader isn't passive, but is asking questions. It is your job to anticipate those questions and to answer them.

Does the ending deliver the promise of the lead?

You made a promise in the lead. Make sure you have completed your contract with the reader.

Rewriting and Editing After Writing

Now the writer steps back and assumes the role of reader. I often role-play a specific person, putting myself in that person's head, and then read the story from their point of view. I pick someone who is intelligent but who does not know or care about the story I have written.

There is a sequence to rewriting and editing from larger to smaller questions. If you do not know, for example, what the story means, then there is no point in moving forward to fix the language. In fact, since language can only be fixed in relation to meaning it is impossible to revise or edit a story without first knowing what it is supposed to mean.

What does the story say?

An effective story has a single dominant message that can be said in a simple sentence. The meaning of the story may have—should have—evolved during the reporting and the writing, but now it is set and that meaning becomes the North Star that guides the writer through all the decisions of rewriting and editing.

Is it worth saying? What would make it worth saying?

Unlike political candidates, we should say something that will serve our readers. If you don't know the significance of the story, you won't be able to make intelligent editorial decisions. Look at the context of the story, the world in which the story exists, to see how the events you are reporting affect that world or the world of your readers.

Is the information in the story accurate in detail and in context?

Reading is an act of trust. When you fail to be trustworthy, you lose a reader—for good.

At *Time,* we were very good at the accuracy of detail and would call an Arab prince at 3:00 A.M. to ask if it was his number three or number four wife and was she wearing real lace, but we were not very good at placing the accurate detail in a proper context. Our task is selection, we choose the fragment to represent the whole. The challenge is to make that representation fair.

Does the form of the story communicate its meaning?

We should not forget that form is meaning. How we design the story—on the basis of chronology, personality, or event—supports what we have to say.

Is the voice of the text appropriate, attractive, and consistent?

We think of voice as belonging to the writer, but what we should do is make sure the voice of the text is tuned so that it clarifies, supports, and communicates the meaning. The read text is the heard text.

Does the story deliver an adequate amount of documented information to the reader? Does the form of the documentation vary according to what is being documented?

The reader has a hunger for information that makes the reader an authority on the subject. Readers read pages that allow them to say, "Hey, did you know that . . . ?"

Is the pace of the story appropriate to the meaning and effective in keeping the reader reading?

See readers' questions below. Each good piece of writing has its own beat, which speeds up or slows down according to what is being said and how it will be heard by the reader.

Are the reader's questions answered when they are asked? Does the story move logically from lead to end?

The effective writer knows where the reader is and what the reader needs to know at any point in the story.

What needs to be added?

Most stories are underdeveloped. They do not give the reader a satisfying serving of specific information.

What needs to be cut?

To get room for that satisfying information, cut and focus. A focussed story has room for depth.

Is each section of the story complete? Does it grow from the previous section and lead the reader to the next section?

Longer stories are constructed from units of meaning that satisfy the reader's need to understand part of the story so that they will be able to understand the next part. It may be helpful to check this by asking how each section answers one question and asks a new one that leads the reader to the next section.

Does each paragraph say one thing and develop and document that meaning?

Each paragraph should deliver information essential to the development of the section.

Does each sentence contain a meaning that is delivered clearly, simply, accurately, and musically?

The sentence is the basic writing unit. Vary your sentences but build on the sentence-verb-object sentence. The declarative sentence is the cornerstone of a clear style. And read your sentences alive. They should flow with music that supports and communicates the meaning of the sentence.

Do the length of paragraphs and sentences vary according to the meaning being communicated (usually short for the points of emphasis or complication, longer for material in between)?

If not, consider their length in terms of their meaning.

Is it possible for the reader to see, hear, touch, smell, and taste the story?

When you can alert a reader's senses, the reader will be drawn into the story.

Do the verbs provide energy to the sentences?

Active verbs are the engines that drive meaning forward.

Are the nouns specific?

The reader's hunger for the specific is rarely satisfied.

Are the adjectives and adverbs necessary?

Of course I use them but never without feeling a tiny sense of failure that I have not found the right noun or verb.

Can the jargon be eliminated? If not, can it be defined immediately, right in the middle of the sentence?

As writers, we have an ear for language. It is easy for us to pick up the jargon and clichés of the people we interview. Watch out.

Is each word the right word?

A word must be right in terms of meaning; it carries its load of information by connotation and denotation.

Are the traditions of our language broken only to clarify meaning?

Language changes under our hands. We accept new forms of language when they communicate meaning with more clarity and grace than traditional usage. Make sure you break traditions when it increases communication.

Does the story follow Globe style?

There is a style book. Use it.

Have you read the story aloud? Does the story read as if a person were talking with the reader or does it read as if it were made by machine?

The ear is the best editor. Read and listen and revise until the text sounds right.

THIRTY THREE

WORKING WITH EDITORS

Although I've been married twice, I find that relationship easier than the one between writer and editor. Writers and editors depend on each other; without the writer there is no copy and without the editor there is no publication. But dependency does not necessarily bring respect or affection, in foreign or personal affairs. In fact, need may cause resentment, suspicion, even combat. Yet there is no divorce during the creation of a story for the next edition; writer and editor have to work together.

Entering the Editor's World

To work well with an editor it is important to practice the reporter's skill of empathy and enter the editor's world. Most writers remind me of a tenor who was listening to the tape playback at an opera recording session. He turned to me and started talking as soon as his last solo was finished. The other performers tried to shush him, but he paid no attention. He told me, "The opera is finished." And it was for him.

The geography of the editor's world includes:
- Many stories that will arrive on deadline or after.
- The fear of blankness—an edition that will be published without anything surrounding the advertisements.
- A superior editor, or editors, who will second-guess every editorial decision.

- An obsession (and an appropriate one) with accuracy in and out of context.
- A comfortable familiarity with journalistic tradition.
- A belief that the writer gets more attention than he or she deserves while the editor labors in obscurity, salvaging the creative attempts of writers.

Each editor's geography will change, but most will have these elements and more. It is important for the writer to know the editor's world and to recognize its landmarks. If you can imagine how your editor views the world, you may be able to make better use of that editor, understanding when to stand clear, when to make contact, and how.

Developing the Editor You Need

Every writer needs at least one editor; most of us need two. One is an assigning or developing editor with whom we can consult before and during the writing. Another is a copy editor who can read with detachment, representing the reader and making sure that the story is clear, graceful, and accurate.

However, the writer's first editor should always be the writer himself or herself. Some writers abdicate this responsibility. In doing this they invite poor editing, for the writer is the reporter and always knows the story, its connotations, and its context better than any editor. The writer needs to develop the ability to make a full commitment to the story and then to stand back and view it from the reader's perspective.

Most times when I write I am able, usually in chunks of four to eight paragraphs, to stand back from the canvas and view my work with detachment. I keep moving into the text and back from it, being uncritical and critical almost simultaneously, but if the critic seems to be winning I always stop standing back and write to the end of the piece, even the chapter, even the book, suspending critical judgment. Writing is an act of faith, and if I have to choose between being a writer and an editor during the creation of a draft, I have no choice. Only by being a writer will I produce a draft that needs an editor.

Working out a relationship with an editor is an extremely tricky business. It is often a matter of personality, and the best way to get around conflicts of personality is to focus on the task at hand: the editing of the text. Few of us can change our personalities, but all of us in this profession have had to learn to work together to produce a daily paper. If we focus on the task, very different personalities can work effectively together.

Once we have established that the text is the focus, then it seems to me that it is the responsibility of the writer to request the editing the writer needs. The editor, of course, has the power to decide if that form of editing is appropriate. But most editors are grateful for clues from the writer as to what the writer needs. An editor, naturally, will handle each story in the manner to which he or she is accustomed. This may lead to severe problems. The writer is concerned about organization, and the editor focuses on usage. Neither will communicate effectively with the other in such a case.

The range of editing a writer needs is extensive; it varies from writer to writer and task to task. Some forms of editing include:

Idea editing

The writer asks himself or herself, then asks the story editor: "What's the focus of the story? What's the dominant idea? What is the one thing the reader will take from the story? How is the story different from the others we've run on the same subject? Why should anyone read this story? What do you expect the reader to think or feel or do after reading the story? What do you think you (and therefore the reader) may learn from the story?

Reporting editing

The writer asks himself or herself, then asks the story editor: "What are the sources I need for this story? What written records are available? Whom should I talk to? Who is responsible for the story? Who is affected by the story? Who is for it? Who is against it? What is the face on the story? Who or what is the force behind the scenes? What is the place of the story? How does the place affect the story?"

Structural editing

The writer asks himself or herself, then asks the story editor: "What is the length of the story? What is its form or genre—profile, straight news, reconstruction, analysis, etcetera? What are the potential leads on the story? What are possible endings? What main points will get the reader from a lead to an end? What are the questions the reader will ask, and in what order will they be asked? What are the proportions of the story—quotation to exposition, anecdote to factual analysis, description to narrative?"

Language editing

The writer asks himself or herself, then asks the story editor: "What is the voice that will communicate the meaning of the story most effectively? What is the effect of balance between long and short sentences and paragraphs? What is the pace of the story and how should it change within the story? What can be cut? What needs to be added? What should be put in a different place? What needs to be clarified? What needs to be documented? What needs to be checked for accuracy?"

Each of us should make up our own checklist for our own editing, and each of us should be able to find an editor from whom we can receive the help we need. Often there is a sequence or timing that is required on each story. This may extend over weeks in a takeout or take place in a few two- or three-minute conferences during an afternoon.

- "I need to talk a little bit about this idea. It's not clear to me how this is different from the last story I did, or if it should be."

- "Now that I've talked to some people I see the story changing. I'd like to talk to you about this."

- "I'd like to try this lead. How about it?"

- "I think this organization works. I've tried to answer the reader's questions when they will be asked. What do you think?"

- "I'm surprised at my tone in this story. Do you think it sounds as if I'm too involved?"

- "I've gotten awfully close to this story. Will you check it to make sure I haven't picked up some jargon that will mean nothing to the reader?"

Most editors will appreciate such requests from the writer. And if they see other problems they can decide whether to mention them now or wait and see if they get solved along the way. The editor, of course, can also make suggestions in the same tone of consultation and professional respect: "I think the piece is well organized. It moves from point to point, but I'm not quite sure about your voice. Listen to the story when you go over it and see if you can help me with that."

The writer, I believe, should take the lead in helping the editor to help the writer. The goal is not for writer or editor to like one another, but to produce an effective story for the reader.

Conflict between editor and writer is probably inevitable. But the writer (or the editor) who is in constant conflict should realize that this is a professional failure. It is the responsibility of each to make sure that they find methods to work together. Each needs the other.

Selling Ideas and New Approaches

The best ideas for stories come, most of the time, from reporters. They are on the street. They hear and see what is going on. Each story should produce other story ideas.

Lively writing—writing that reveals the meaning of the story in a way that attracts and serves readers—is also the principal responsibility of the reporter/writer. A well-written story is the responsibility of the writer.

One of the big problems is that the editor thrives on predictability more than most editors care to admit. Editors, their backs to deadline, are not usually prepared for surprises. Yet the best stories surprise the reader with the information in the story, or the way the information is prescribed, or both.

The challenge is to get the surprise to the editor in such a way that it is not a surprise. Whenever there is time I strongly urge that the writer make a proposal in writing. My own formula for such a proposal is one that I have used as a freelance magazine and book writer, and it has been used by editors as a model for other writers.

It doesn't take much time to write, but it has enormous benefits for both writer and editor. Here is what I do.

- I write the title or head that *may* appear on the final story. I realize that in a newspaper this may not be the headline on the final version. It is, however, important for me to focus the story, to compress its meaning into a few words. And it helps the editor to see that focus. I used the title "Over Sixty" when I proposed my column for the *Globe*. It defined my audience and point of view for me and for the editors who considered the column. I have found it a good investment to write a head on a proposal.

- I write the lead, the first ten lines or so, that *may* appear in the story. I may have to make up an anecdote, or quote, or scene, even some facts, but I am not writing a contract. I am writing a proposal. I want to see the story as a reader may see it, and I want the editor to see that potential story. And I find that a lead, which includes the focus, the tone, and, by implication, the whole shape and length of the story, is the best way to do it.

- I indent and use bullets or bold boxes, as I have here, to indicate the three to five main points of the story. I keep them short, tight, and specific. As in the lead, I am not tentative, and I reveal each point in a few lines as it may be revealed to the reader. In the case of a book I use a chapter title and about five lines under it to show the editor the dimensions and the sequence of the material in the book.

- I write a final paragraph in which I tell the editor what the editor needs to know; for example, if I have access to the sources in the story, if there is a special reason for the story to be published, if there is a special audience for the story, if there is a possibility for special art, or whatever. I do not lecture the editor, saying that this story should be published because . . . I try to make those reasons obvious through the information that I have presented to the editor.

I write these proposals single spaced and try to keep them on one page, except when I am proposing a book. I find that the written proposal is far more effective than an oral one. When I talk an idea through, the chance is that the editor hears something different than what I thought the editor heard, and I hear something different from the editor's response than the editor intended. When I have a written text, it forces me to be much clearer in my proposal. I have to anticipate and solve problems. This procedure allows the editor to respond in a much more disciplined way, to propose alternatives, to identify problems, and to make productive suggestions.

The editor who has received such a written proposal may become a supporter of a radically different story than the writer would have expected. The editor may see, for example, that this story needs to be a narrative, or that it has to be written entirely in dialogue, or that it is appropriate to see the story from only one point of view. Such surprises can be sold best when they are sold in writing and when the editor has seen, perhaps only in a paragraph or two, the demonstration of an approach that is different but appropriate to revealing the true significance of the story.

We should always remember that. We do not want surprises for surprise's sake, liveliness just to be lively, but we should always aim to reveal the significance of the story. Too often that significance is hidden under the clichés of journalism. It is the responsibility of the writer and editor, in that order, to find ways to report and write stories so they deliver the information the reader needs to know.

The Community of Writer/Readers

Writing is a lonely business, even in the City Room. In my case, I literally work alone, and publication, in the case of books, may come a year or more after a draft is done. I need a small community of readers from whom I can get an immediate response.

I have developed my own community of writer/readers. Most important is Chip Scanlan of the Knight-Ridder Washington Bureau, for which the telephone company should be grateful. My other readers are in New Hampshire (two), Massachusetts, Maine, Wyoming, Idaho, and Ohio. Nine in all, but some have a husband, wife, or partner reader, so I often get two for the price of one. These are the people for whom I write and from whom I get responses I trust and depend on.

If you are creating your own community of writer/readers, you may be interested in the qualities mine share.

- They all write. They know the territory. They know how it feels to write. I can share writing in progress and they know where I am in the writing process and the response that will be helpful at that time.

- They can enter into my copy and see what I am trying to do. Too many editors impose external standards. My readers help me fulfill my own goals in my own way.

- They tell me what works as well as what needs work. They are honest but supportive.

- They listen to my garumphs—my fears, my doubts, my problems, my complaints—and they share theirs with me.

THIRTY FOUR

Interview:
EVELYNNE KRAMER

I need editing and I've learned to cultivate editors. I have my horror stories, but they have been rare. On the other hand, working with editors who can get inside my writing and really help me has been equally rare.

Mort Howell, adviser to the newspaper I edited my freshman year in college, could do that. He didn't make me write his text but helped me realize my own. Eddie Devin, assistant city editor on the old *Boston Herald,* was another. Bob Johnson, for whom I wrote my first articles for *The Saturday Evening Post,* and Walter Ross of *Coronet* were others. Linda Buchanan Allen, now a writer but formerly an editor at Houghton Mifflin, was another editor who taught me. And now I have Evelynne Kramer. Six superb editors in forty-seven years. I've been lucky.

Remember, I've had hundreds of newspaper, magazine, and book editors who have supported and encouraged me, who have saved me from law suits, ridicule, and shame. I've had a few other editors with whom I would have evolved a special relationship if we worked together long enough or if we faced a turning point in my career together. One is Toby Gordon, with whom I am working at Heinemann. But here I'm talking about editors on my wave length whose editing stimulates me to write better than I have before, who give me the freedom to go beyond my normal limits because I know they will catch me if I fall, who teach me to write.

These editors have different styles, and so have I. I've kept growing as a writer and I have different needs according to where I am and according to the writing task I face. And that is where I start with a new editor. I tell the editor I need editing and welcome it, but I go on to describe the stages in the writing process when I need it and the kind of editing I prefer.

Once I start working with an editor, I tell the editor (and often the editor's boss) why I like working with that person and I do it in specific terms: "She's able to help me hear my own voice."

I've met stupid editors, editors I regret not tossing out a window on the twenty-seventh floor of the Time/Life Building, but I believe the writing/editing relationship is collaborative. We need each other and it is my job as well as the editor's to make that relationship work.

It works with Evelynne Kramer. She is a professional. She was graduated from Syracuse University and worked at the *Syracuse Herald-Journal,* the *Binghamton Evening Press,* the *Daily Hampshire Gazette,* and the *Springfield Union* before joining the *Boston Globe,* where she has held many jobs including city editor, State House editor, City Hall editor, regional editor, and an editor of Focus.

What do you know about editing now that you wish you had known when you began editing?

I think editing requires patience and that editors need to think about long-term goals with a writer—not just working with the story that's on the screen. We can all get better at what we do, but improvement sometimes takes a lot of time and more often than not, some fits and starts. Patience, alas, has never been my long suit; it's something I've had to work on.

I have also learned that nobody wants to hear what's wrong with a story before he or she hears what's right with it. It's sometimes easy for editors to forget that under the press of deadlines, but I think learning to focus on what works in a story is critical to building an effective relationship with a writer.

I depend on hearing that you think a column or a feature works before you go through the copy with me. I smile because I know the pattern, but I confess that I need it. I know what may be wrong better than I know what works. Will you describe how the editor's role changes as you move from giving an assignment to editing final copy? What is the most important editing skill at each stage?

During the assignment, an editor needs to be able to communicate the premise of a story, but that's only half of it. The editor also needs to listen to the writer's ideas, to sort out what the writer thinks the story might be, and even to be prepared to change the direction of a story totally.

Figuring out how an assignment is proceeding also calls on the editor to listen, concentrate, and respond with confidence to new information. What surprises the editor can be a clue to how to structure the story or how to write the lead.

The final editing of a story takes what we used to call pencil skills— the ability to see what the writer is up to and to help the writer achieve that on his or her own terms. It all has to make sense to the reader, of course, or it's all for naught.

Once you suggested that I toss out a column and start over. It was done so gracefully that I got all excited about writing a new draft. How do you deliver bad news so the writer isn't discouraged and will be motivated to revise or do better next time?

As an editor, that's one of the hardest things to learn to do, and many times I have not done it as gracefully as I should.

The first step is to reassure the writer that it is all going to turn out alright, that you are an ally in the process, and that you are not going to leave the writer hanging out to dry, even if—as was the case in your column—you think a complete rewrite is needed. Writers also need to know that you have confidence in their ability, and that you and the writer are in it together.

I have learned a lot about giving feedback from my music teacher. First, you have to understand that I have no musical talent even though I have enjoyed fooling around with the piano for years. Bruce, my teacher, somehow encourages me to keep going, to try again even when I have screwed up badly. Part of his technique is to find something I did right and comment on it. Then, he can launch into a discussion, usually long, of what I did wrong.

I've talked about the attitudes I try to bring to the editor/writer relationship. What attitudes do you hope the editor will bring to the editor/writer encounter?

I think it is important for the editor to respect the writer and to communicate that respect honestly and clearly. Respect is independent of whether you agree or disagree about an approach to a story.

And what attitudes do you hope the writer will bring to the editor/writer encounter?

Ditto. I think it is important for writers to respect their editors. I don't know as much about the subject matter as any of the writers I work with, but I hope I know something about editing, and that can help the writer and ultimately the reader.

All my writing life I have suffered from editors who bring preconceptions to the reading of my copy that make the editing a nightmare. They know what they expect and cannot read what I'm trying to do on its own terms, in its own context, in its own voice. You are just the opposite. You are one of the few who are able to read my copy on its own terms and make suggestions within my context and voice. How do you do this?

Accepting a writer's voice has a lot to do with accepting a writer. It's really about accepting people for who they are, not what you want them to be. What more can I say about this? When it comes right down to it, this has a lot to do with learning to accept yourself, and that's a lifelong task. I'm better at it now than I used to be.

As I've also said, I try to respond to editors and let them know what works for me. What response do you think editors need from writers?

I think editors need to hear when they have done something right, when they've improved a story, come up with a good idea, or helped a writer get better. Editors need encouragement almost as much as writers; if writers want their editors to be there for them, they need to tell them when they've done something right.

You've been responsible for many lively stories in Food, At Home, and Living recently, including a couple of mine I would never have thought of writing. What are the elements of a good story idea? What techniques do you have for fitting writer to idea or vice versa? How do you encourage ideas from writers?

A good story surprises the reader. A good story idea surprises me. It's been a lot of fun to encourage some new thinking about the kind of story that belongs in Food and At Home. I like to think most of us can write from our own lives from time to time, and I like to encourage writers to think about their own experiences as a starting point. Some of the most talked-about stories we've done in these sections (Nick King's piece on single dads comes to mind) were born over a casual conversation about ordinary activities.

Our readers need to laugh and they need to see themselves in the newspaper. I would like to think they can do both in these sections.

You've certainly helped me sharpen many leads. Let's talk about leads: What do you like in a lead? Dislike? What's often missing? How can an editor or writer sharpen a lead?

A lead is an invitation to read on. Sometimes, the story calls for a clearly written hard news approach; sometimes, a more leisurely pace. It's hard to generalize, but I thing an effective lead makes me want to know more. Taking a second look at a lead minutes, or hours, later can help you see something that was missing or help you fix a phrase that falls flat. It's that second reading that's really helpful.

I'm especially grateful for the help you've given me in revealing a word that isn't right and, far more difficult, in helping me hear where the music of my writing falters in a phrase or a line. How have you trained yourself to read with such care? Do you read aloud? What do you do so you can hear the draft?

I think most editors develop an ear with practice. If I sense a problem with a sentence, I read it over several times very slowly, sometimes aloud, to try to figure out where it breaks down. Interestingly, many writers are not surprised when you point to a paragraph that is a clunker. They already may have had a sense that something wasn't working.

What do you do when you read a draft that has serious organizational problems? What tricks of your trade have you developed to bring order to chaos or to help the writer bring order to chaos?

If I sense a problem, I usually try to break the story down into an outline—to see the parts of a whole. Then I try to figure out whether there is a logical progression of ideas—whether my questions get answered as they come to me. If they don't I am likely to suggest a refiguring of the piece.

I hate to admit it, but I live for your praise. I'm not proud of being a dancing bear, but I am. Will you say something about the importance of telling a writer what works as well as what doesn't work and how an editor can do it?

There is always something that works with a story, and that is a good starting point, as I've said. It's important for an editor to be honest about this, though, because false praise serves neither the writer nor editor. Writers can see right through it, and that can damage your credibility pretty quickly. You've got to focus on something that really does distinguish the piece and go from there.

THIRTY FIVE

Interview:
FAMOUS WRITERS
LIVING AND DEAD

I was apprenticed to our craft when Miss Chapman, my fourth-grade teacher, looked down on me from her enormous height and commanded, "Donald, you are the editor of the class newspaper." When I was in North Quincy Junior High I abandoned the branch library in Wollaston and discovered the open stacks at the main Quincy Library. While searching, mostly unsuccessfully, for books on s-e-x I found books on writing; books about writers; foreign correspondents, and journalists; books by writers. I started a commonplace book, years before I ever heard that term, writing down quotations by writers about writing. Now I have published a collection of quotations on writing called *Shoptalk: Learning to Write with Writers.* It was developed from the thousands of quotations I had collected through the years and this interview will be with some of those writers from whom I have learned writing.

What are you looking for when you go out on a story?
The writer is looking for the informing material. —*Maxine Kumin*

Have you had any assignments when there was no story?
I blame myself for not often enough seeing the extraordinary in the ordinary. Somewhere in his journals Dostoyevsky remarks that a writer can begin anywhere, at the most commonplace thing, scratch around in it

long enough, pry and dig away long enough, and, lo!, soon he will hit upon the marvelous. —*Saul Bellow*

What do you think has made you an effective reporter?
Curiosity urges you on—the driving force. —*John Dos Passos*

Will you describe how you work as a reporter?
The writer . . . sees what he did not expect to see. . . . Inattentive learner in the schoolroom of life, he keeps some faculty free to hear and wonder. His is the roving eye. By that roving eye is his subject found. The glance, at first only vaguely caught, goes on to concentrate, deepen; becomes the vision. —*Elizabeth Bowen*

What advice do you have for a beginning reporter on the Globe?
Try to be one of the people on whom nothing is lost. —*Henry James*

What about your relationship to your sources?
Isn't disloyalty as much the writer's virtue as loyalty is the soldier's? —*Graham Greene*

Why did you become a writer in the first place?
I began to write because I was too shy to talk, and too lonely not to send messages. —*Heather McHugh*

You can write fast food stories on deadline when you have to but the stories that have won awards are different. You and Wil Haygood have that special quality. Can you describe it?
I strive for imperfection, for that rawness, clumsiness, an awkwardness—which retains an energy—so hard to do. Perfection is the death of energy. —*Walter Abish*

Could you describe that again?
To write well, one needs a natural facility and an acquired difficulty. —*Joubert*

One editor mentioned your ability at rewrite. What do you do?
The greatest artist is the simplifier. —*Henri Frederic Amiel*

I'm impressed at how you can take an ordinary police story or a hearing at city hall and give it a special quality. How do you do that?
A sentence is born both good and bad at the same time. The whole

secret lies in a barely perceptible twist. The control handle must be warm in your hand. You must turn it only once, never twice. —*Isaac Babel*

But it doesn't seem tricky, what you do. How do you keep from getting between the reader and the story, from getting in the way?

The hardest thing about writing, in a sense, is not writing. I mean, the sentence is not designed to show you off, you know. It is not supposed to be "look at me!" "look, no hands!" It's supposed to be a pipeline between the reader and you. One condition of the sentence is to write so well that no one notices that you're writing. —*James Baldwin*

Your writing seems so, well, natural.

It takes a great deal of experience to become natural. —*Willa Cather*

Did you study style?

I never study style; all that I do is try to get the subject as clear as I can in my own head, and express it in the commonest language which occurs to me. —*Charles Darwin*

How would you describe the writing you like?

A good style in literature, if closely examined, will be seen to consist in a constant succession of tiny surprises. —*Ford Maddox Ford*

What other qualities do you see in the best writing in the Globe?

Vigorous writing is concise. A sentence should contain no unnecessary words, a paragraph no unnecessary sentences, for the same reason that a drawing should have no unnecessary lines and a machine no unnecessary parts. This requires not that the writer make all his sentences short, or that he avoid all detail and treat his subjects only in outline, but that every word tell. —*William Strunk*

As a reporter you seem to be able to find the revealing detail and build your stories from those significant specifics.

The more particular, the more specific you are, the more universal you are. —*Nancy Hale*

When I read your writing, I seem to hear it. How do you get that quality in your articles?

I still read everything aloud. I have a fundamental conviction that if a sentence cannot be read aloud with sincerity, conviction, and communicable emphasis, it is not a good sentence. Good writing requires good rhythms and good words. You cannot know whether the rhythms and the words are good unless you read them aloud. Reading aloud is also the easiest way to see that prose tracks, that it runs on smoothly from sentence to sentence, idea to idea, section to section within the larger whole. Reading aloud also makes the mind consider connotations of words and perhaps above all their relations to each other. —*Richard Marius*

How do you proceed to write a story?

I don't write a *word* of the article until I have the lead. It just sets the whole tone—the whole point of view. I know exactly where I'm going as soon as I have the lead. —*Nora Ephron*

Sometimes, I can't get started writing immediately. Does that ever happen to you?

Delay is natural to a writer. He is like a surfer—he bides his time, waits for the perfect wave on which to ride in. Delay is instinctive with him. He waits for the surge (of emotion? of strength? of courage?) that will carry him along. —*E. B. White*

Is that writer's block?

There is no such thing as writer's block. My father drove a truck for 40 years. And never once did he wake up in the morning and say: "I have truckdriver's block today. I am not going to work." —*Roger Simon*

What rituals do you have to get started?

Rituals? Ridiculous! My only ritual is to sit close enough to the typewriter so that my fingers touch the keys. —*Isaac Asimov*

Let's go back to when you've finished your reporting and are on deadline.

I try to write without consulting my material; this avoids interruption and prevents me from overloading my text with quotations. In this way, I establish a comfortable distance from the mass and pressure of data. It helps the narrative flow; it is a guard against irrelevancies. —*Leon Edel*

Any other tricks while writing on deadline?

Too often I wait for the sentence to finish taking shape in my mind before setting it down. It is better to seize it by the end that first offers itself, head and foot, though not knowing the rest, then pull: the rest will follow along. —*André Gide*

Do you organize your stories?

I want to get the structural problems out of the way first, so I can get to what matters more. After they're solved, the only thing left for me to do is tell the story as well as possible. At that point, there is no escape. I'm just dealing with words on paper. —*John McPhee*

What about organizing a complicated story?

If in the first chapter you say that a gun hung on the wall, in the second or third chapter it must without fail be discharged. —*Anton Chekhov*

Do you follow your plan?

Follow the accident, fear the fixed plan—that is the rule. —*John Fowles*

How do you document your stories so readers will keep reading?

The writer makes his living by anecdotes. He searches them out and carves them as the raw materials of his profession. No hunter stalking his prey is more alert to the presence of his quarry than a writer looking for small incidents that cast a strong light on human behavior . . . very little has meaning to the writer except as it is tied to the reality of a single person, and except as that reality can illustrate a larger lesson or principle. —*Norman Cousins*

Don't you get tired of fiddling with your language?

Working at sentences and rhythms is probably the most satisfying thing I do as a writer. I think after a while a writer can begin to know himself through his language. He sees someone or something reflected back at him from these constructions. Over the years it's possible for a writer to shape himself as a human being through the language he uses. I think written language, fiction, goes that deep. He not only sees himself but begins to make himself or remake himself. —*Don Delillo*

Then you care about grammar.

What I know about grammar is its infinite power. To shift the structure of a sentence alters the meaning of that sentence, as definitely and inflexibly as the position of a camera alters the meaning of the object photographed. Many people know about camera angles now, but not so many know about sentences. —*Joan Didion*

Any rules you have found that are particularly helpful?

Writing simply means no dependent clauses, no dangling things, no flashbacks, and keeping the subject near the predicate. We throw in as many fresh words as we can get away with. Simple, short sentences don't always work. You have to do tricks with pacing, alternate long sentences with short, to keep it vital and alive. Virtually every page is a cliffhanger—you've got to force them to turn it. —*Theodor Geisel (Dr. Seuss)*

That's all?

The adjective is the enemy of the noun. —*Voltaire*

How do you know the writing is going well?

When I see a paragraph shrinking under my eyes like a strip of bacon in a skillet, I know I'm on the right track. —*Peter DeVries*

That doesn't sound very spontaneous, yet your writing has that spontaneous quality.

In my own case there are days when the result is so bad that no fewer than five revisions are required. However, when I'm greatly inspired, only four revisions are needed before, as I've often said, I put in that note of spontaneity which even my meanest critics concede. —*John Kenneth Galbraith*

Have you had any difficulty with editors?

No passion in the world is equal to the passion to alter someone else's draft. —*H. G. Wells*

What's the most difficult problem you've had?

A poet can survive anything but a misprint. —*Oscar Wilde*

Is writing easy for you?

A writer is a person for whom writing is more difficult than it is for other people. —*Thomas Mann*

Still you keep writing?

As late as 1806 I was waiting for genius to descend upon me so that I might write. . . . If I had spoken around 1795 of my plan to write, some sensible man would have told me "to write every day for an hour or two."

Genius or no genius. That advice would have made me use ten years of my life that I spent stupidly waiting for genius. —*Stendhal*

You must be very disciplined.

Writing a book is like rearing children—willpower has very little to do with it. If you have a little baby crying in the middle of the night, and if you depend only on willpower to get you out of bed to feed the baby, that baby will starve. You do it out of love. —*Annie Dillard*

What advice do you have to young writers on the Globe?

There is no mystery about art. Do the things that you can see, they will show you those that you cannot see. By doing what you can you will gradually get to know what it is that you want to do and cannot do, and so be able to do it. —*Samuel Butler*

But we said a writer should learn to be natural. How do you find out what is natural for you?

To be nobody-but-yourself—in a world which is doing its best, night and day, to make you everybody else—means to fight the hardest battle which any human being can fight; and never stop fighting.
—*e. e. cummings*

But what if the editors don't like natural?

You have to remember that nobody every wants a new writer. You have to create your own demand. —*Doris Lessing*

What do you think of that writer on the staff—we know the one— who calls attention to himself by his style?

His overpowering impulse is to gyrate before his fellow man, flapping his wings and emitting defiant yells. This being forbidden by the police of all civilized countries, he takes it out by putting his yells on paper. Such is the thing called self-expression. —*H. L. Mencken*

How do you think the Globe could improve its writing?

Let the speech be short, comprehending much in few words.
—*Ecclesiastes*

HOW TO KEEP
LEARNING TO WRITE

I am never bored and, in my late sixties, I haven't burned out. Each morning there is a new page to write and in that page what I didn't know I knew. I live in surprise because I practice a craft that can never be learned. The writer is blessed with an eternal apprenticeship.

The greatest danger the newswriter faces is the achievement of competence—the practice of accomplished, reliable, predictable mediocrity. Editors depend on such competence, but the writer should push beyond the professional demands of most newsrooms and continue to study the never-learned craft of writing.

The first rewards of craft are selfish: the opportunity for concentration and escape from life when the writer becomes lost in the work, the making sense of your individual life, the joy of creating a piece of writing that stands up to a critical eye, the satisfaction of being heard, the independence that comes from being able to deliver. And, as writers practice their craft, they participate in the making of the world; writers educate, stimulate, influence, and persuade.

A writer is not judged on contacts, a selling smile, the color of the writer's skin, sex, or age but on the words on the page. What has been published does not count; each work is the product of a beginner. That rule is harsh, liberating, and challenging.

Here are some of the ways I continue to learn my craft:

Sharing my work in process with colleagues invites them to share their work with me; teaching those who are new to our craft allows me to learn from them. As I listen to their solving of their own writing problems, I add new tricks to my repertoire. And in teaching, I have to learn what I know, to define what I do by instinct. In doing this I become more aware of my own craft.

Seeing my world anew. Cézanne said, "I could keep myself busy for months without moving from one spot, just by leaning now to the right, now to the left." James Baldwin said, "The importance of a writer . . . is that he is here to describe things which other people are too busy to describe." I try to keep myself open to my world by moving the angle of vision so that the familiar becomes strange.

Empathy allows me to enter the skin of others and to live other lives. I am cop and crook, senator and voter, corporate executive and laborer, soldier and pacifist, abortionist and member of Operation Rescue, black and white, Christian and Jew, young and old, male and female, heterosexual and homosexual, country and city, native and emigré. That is the necessary arrogance of the writer who passes in imagination through many worlds, learning what needs to be investigated, what questions need to be asked.

Reading makes me familiar with the best writers, past and present, and their lessons infiltrate my craft. Reading writers better than I am should make me quit, but instead I am inspired, not to compete, but to practice our discipline. The newswriter should read the best journalists, as well as poets, short-story writers, novelists, playwrights, screenwriters, and essayists. Journalists should also see films to see how scenes are revealed and read historians to discover how the past may be kept alive, anthropologists to discover how human life can be documented, scientists to learn precision of vision, and naturalists to know how to celebrate our natural world. Writers should also read the interviews, critical essays, diaries, notebooks, autobiographies, and biographies of writers, artists, and composers to understand the artistic life and the artistic craft.

Reinventing ourselves as writers is important to our growth. Cross-genre writing is as profitable as cross-training. Our news stories will be better written because of our experiments with poetry, fiction, or screen writing. We should try to write opinion for the op-ed page or the arts section and articles for the Sunday magazine; explore the possibility of writing for business and living and sports and politics and the courts; and attempt profiles, hard news, exposés, mood pieces, and human interest. Writers have a blessed flexibility denied to most editors.

Research allows the writer to enter the laboratory and Congress, corporate board room and hospital operating room, AIDS clinic and police holding cell, opera green room and football dressing room. The writer should be student to the world. But research should also lead writers into themselves, exploring with memory the territories of childhood, school, war, and social relationships to discover the central mysteries of their lives. Those mysteries can be explored by writing that, when written, will articulate the unspoken thoughts and feelings of readers. If writers do this, they discover that the more personal we are, the more universal our writing becomes.

Writing itself is the best way to become, again and again, young at the writing desk. Each draft of the most familiar assignment provides the possibility for learning. As Tom Williams, the novelist, told me, "The writer should always have a private experiment in each piece of writing. The reader may never know what it is, but the writer will." And the writer will learn from that private challenge. The most simple experiments of craft may produce the most interesting possibilities: Try the present tense; experiment with scene and narrative; cut the draft in half; double its length; tell it all in dialogue; only use description; stand far back; move in close; write in the first person or the third; write it funny, sad, nostalgic; amuse, persuade, expose, document. The possibilities have not yet ended for me in more than four years of column writing and in the other genre I explore.

Risk is the safest road for the writer to take. All we can be sure of in this life is change. After I won the Pulitzer at age twenty-nine, people said I was set with the paper for life. That paper does not exist. I went to *Time* and learned more by failing than I would have with success. I freelanced for magazines that are no longer published, had novels accepted and rejected, poems taken and poems sent back in the next mail. I wrote a book on teaching before I knew how to teach and helped start a movement in the teaching of writing because I was ignorant of what could not be done. Every time I have risked, I have done well; when I have gone with the sure thing it hasn't been sure. Writing, after all, is always a risk—of ignorance, of self-exposure, of writing what others will not applaud.

Play is the central process of our craft. Study what you have done when the writing has gone well and emphasize that until you come to the writing desk with confidence, eager to begin the play with language that will reveal the world and make your craft your avocation and vocation.

Produce. E. L. Doctorow says, "the writing generates the writing." If you want to be a writer, write. Do not plan to write, think about writing, read about writing, talk about writing; write. Write what is at hand—news stories, press releases, ghost speeches, brochures, poems, essays, editorials, columns, novels, short stories, songs, plays, television and movie scripts—what you have the opportunity to write, and what you dream of writing. The "writing generates the writing"; the more you write, the more you will write.

Listen to yourself above all, write what *you* need to write in the way *you* need to write it. Pay attention to teachers, editors, colleagues, critics, and readers—but not too much attention. I have learned from all of them, but I have also paid too much attention to most of them, following advice that was good for others but disastrous for me. When the Prince Regent's librarian asked Jane Austen to write a romance, she responded, "No, I must keep to my own style, and go on in my own way; and though I may never succeed *again* in that, I am convinced that I should totally fail in any other." Gertrude Stein said, "No artist needs criticism, he only needs appreciation. If he needs criticism he is not an artist." I began by advising writers to share, and I close by saying that after all the sharing, listen most of all to yourself.

Be grateful you lead the writer's life, working alone at a craft that can never be learned.

GLOSSARY

Attribution Information in a news story should not float free. It should be anchored to a source so the reader knows where the information comes from. Information can, of course, be attributed to the reporter.

Backgrounder A story that gives the reader the history or context of a news event.

Billboard Another term for a nut graph.

Cliché of language A cliché is an expression that might have once been bright and new, but has become worn with use like an old slipper, so it can fit any foot. The cliché has been used by so many people in so many different ways that it no longer helps the reader see or understand.

Cliché of vision If we don't watch out, we begin to see what we expect to see, not what we really see. The fullback always charges; the survivor always grieves. We need to train ourselves to observe so that the familiar is not.

Closure The reader needs to feel a sense of completeness at the end of a story, that all the reader's questions have been asked even if they can't all be answered.

Explainers News room jargon for stories that attempt to go further back and further forward than the conventional news story, explaining the meaning of a story for the reader.

Face A news story that is told in terms of an individual person—the crime wave that is described in the terms of a single victim.

Folo A story that follows-up or reports developments in a breaking news story.

Hard news Information the reader needs to know immediately.

Inverted pyramid stories Traditional news stories that tell the reader the most important news first, the next important news next, and so on. If space is needed, these stories can be cut from the bottom right up to the lead paragraph, which is packed with the most important information.

Kicker A strong ending on a news story, column, or editorial; information that will make an impact on the reader and remain with the reader after the story is finished.

Layering The process of writing a story over and over again to develop it adequately.

Lead (or lede) Information that will make the reader want to read on, that will lead the reader into the story. **Delayed lead** This is a lead that doesn't give all the information to the reader immediately, but usually gives a specific—an anecdote, a scene, a quotation—and then puts the specific incident into context, usually in the third or fourth paragraph. **Hard news lead** The reader is given the information the reader needs as soon as possible and in the order the reader needs it. **Soft delayed lead** (Same as delayed lead).

The Line A fragment of language that contains the central tension that will move a story forward.

Mapping A brainstorming technique in which the writer puts a topic in the center of the page and then, as rapidly as possible, draws branches out to any topics that seem related.

Natural order A story that uses a sequence that seems normal to organize the information for the reader. Chronology is used in a narrative; sometimes a place is described by taking a walk through it. Often a legislative act is shown by allowing the reader to experience the process of getting a bill passed or blocked.

New journalism A term used to describe the journalism of the late sixties and seventies, in which the reporter/writer abandoned the position of objective observer and participated in the story and commented upon the story with personal opinion.

News hole The amount of space left after the advertising columns have been allocated.

Nut graph A paragraph that follows the lead and puts the story in context.

Point of view Sometimes used to describe the opinion of the writer, other times used to describe the place from which the reader is allowed to view the story.

Roundup A story that summarizes all that has been written on a story that has been appearing in the paper over a period of time.

Sidebar A subsidiary story that runs beside a main story.

Takeout A story that attempts to put an entire issue in context.

Traditional journalism Journalism in which the reporter emphasizes fact, makes no comment upon it, does not intrude on the story, and maintains a position as an objective, impartial deliverer of attributed information.

2-3-1 principle A way of describing the points of emphasis in a unit of writing. The most important point is at the end, the next important point at the beginning, and the least in the middle.

VDT Visual Display Terminal, one of the terms used to describe the word processors on which reporters write their stories and have them edited.

Voice The quality of writing, sometimes called style or tone, that gives the reader the illusion of an individual person speaking to an individual reader.

RECOMMENDED READING

This is obviously a brief, personal selection.

Blundell, William E., *Storytelling Step by Step* (Dow Jones & Company, 1986). (I believe a trade version is now available.)

Clark, Roy Peter and Don Fry. A new book on coaching in the newsroom to be published shortly.

Franklin, Jon, *Writing for Story* (Atheneum, 1986).

Harrigan, Jane, *Read All About It! A Day in the Life of a Metropolitan Newspaper* (Globe Pequot Press, 1987).

Jerome, John, *The Writing Trade—A Year in the Life* (Viking, 1992). The best book I know on writing nonfiction. Wise, candid, realistic, inspiring. Jerome practices the craft he preaches.

McPhee, John, *The John McPhee Reader,* William Howarth ed. (Random House, Vintage Books, 1976). This book includes an extensive description of his working methods. Any book by McPhee is a class in nonfiction writing.

Murray, Donald M., *A Writer Teaches Writing* (Houghton Mifflin, 1968, 1985).

———*Learning by Teaching,* 2nd edition (Heinemann, Boynton/Cook, 1989).

———*Write to Learn,* 4th edition (Harcourt Brace Jovanovich, 1993).

———*Read to Write,* 3rd edition (Harcourt Brace Jovanovich, 1993).

——— *Expecting the Unexpected* (Heinemann, Boynton/Cook, 1989).

——— *Shoptalk, Learning to Write with Writers* (Heinemann, Boynton/Cook, 1990).

——— *The Craft of Revision* (Harcourt Brace Jovanovich, 1991).

Poynter Institute, *Best Newspaper Writing—The American Society of Newspaper Editors Competition* (The Poynter Institute, 1981).

Sims, Norman, *The Literary Journalists* (Ballantine Books, 1984).

Strunk, William, Jr., and E. B. White, *The Elements of Style,* 3rd edition (Macmillan, 1979).

Witt, Len, *The Complete Book of Feature Writing* (Writer's Digest Press, 1991).

Writers at Work—the Paris Review Interviews, Vols. 1–6, various editors (Viking [hardcover], Penguin).

Zinsser, William, *On Writing Well: An Informal Guide to Writing Nonfiction,* 4th edition (HarperCollins, 1990).

INDEX

About the Author

Donald M. Murray, who was chosen as best columnist in Boston in 1991 by *Boston Magazine,* won the Pulitzer Prize for editorial writing on *The Boston Herald* in 1954. He has served as writing coach for *The Boston Globe, The Providence Journal,* and other newspapers. His weekly column, "Over Sixty," appears in *The Boston Globe.* In addition to working as a journalist, Murray has published two novels, and his poems have appeared in many journals, including *Poetry.*

A pioneer of the writing-process movement in education, Murray's books on writing include *A Writer Teaches Writing, Learning by Teaching, Write to Learn, Read to Write, Expecting the Unexpected, Shoptalk, Learning to Write with Writers,* and *The Craft of Revision.*

Murray is professor emeritus of English at the University of New Hampshire, where he inaugurated a journalism program, designed an advanced composition course, and helped establish a graduate program in composition studies. He twice won awards for his teaching.